Self Publish for *FREE*

Step by Step

Self Publish for *FREE*

Step by Step

John Rehg

Fiction and Memoir Edition

Soul Attitude Press

Published by Soul Attitude Press, Pinellas Park, Florida.
Visit the publisher's web site: www.soulattitudepress.com.

Cover design by John Rehg
Cover art from openclipart.org courtesy dear_theophilus
a librarian http://www.inkylabs.com/~sarato

Photo for Zombieween cover: Brianna Weiss, copyright © 2015 by Brianna Weiss.
Make-up by Brianna Weiss.

Materials from J Gerard Michaels and Tic Rawghers used with permission.

Arrow used in Bonus section courtesy rg1024 from openclipart.org
http://rg1024.wordpress.com/category/openclipart/

Volume 1 of the Step by Step series: Fiction and Memoir

ISBN: 978-1-939181-70-1

FIRST EDITION

Printed in the United States of America

Table of Contents

Dedication

To Chi, who has stood with me and encouraged me in all my endeavors, and helped with the cover design. To Mom and Dad, and my brothers and sisters, who have served as reviewers and/or supporters of my writing. To Cate Bronson and Bria Burton of The Fab Four critique group, who have offered helpful insights and suggestions.

And to the open source community and many on the Internet who have offered tutorials and instructions on how to use the software. It has saved me a tremendous amount of time.

How to Use This Book

Buttons to be clicked, or menu items that you would click on to access a function are *italicized*.

Descriptions of some images are included in blue boxes if they go beyond just naming the picture. Captions are not boxed in.

On some pages you'll see a box at the bottom titled: The Fine Print. Some of these will expand on the instructions, some will hold my opinion on the subject, others will offer encouragement.

Most instructions will be the same for several versions leading up to the one used in this book. Some minor differences are noted where they were found.

Your Questions Answered

What will this book do for me?

This book will show you step-by-step how to prepare your own book for publishing, using free software. The only cost, other than for this guide, would be when you purchase the book you've published.

Why buy this book when there are plenty of instructions, videos, tutorials, etc. on the Internet?

To give you, in one place, all you need to publish your story.

Who will publish my book?

Amazon's on demand publisher, CreateSpace.

What if I get into trouble with the software?

If you find something particularly vexxing, shoot me an email at soulattitudepress@gmail.com. Or post a comment on the website. There will be a post about this book, and that's where questions will be answered. In addition, there are forums for all the free software where people can help.

Is there an easier way to do this?

Yes, there is! Sort of. CreateSpace gives you templates for your document, a free ISBN number and barcode, and has an online cover creator where you can create your cover in 5 minutes.

Why not do it the easier way?

The tradeoff is that you give up some control over the look of your product. Also, what looks to be easier, can actually be more difficult. I'll explain in the following chapters.

Your Recipe for Success

Ingredients:

1 Word Processor   LibreOffice Writer - Version 5.0.1
> Download: http://www.libreoffice.org/download/libreoffice-fresh/

1 Layout Program   Scribus - Version 1.4.5
> Download: http://wiki.scribus.net/canvas/Download

1 Graphics Program   GIMP - Version 2.8.14
> Download: http://www.gimp.org/downloads/

Substitutions:

Word Processor: Microsoft (MS) Word, WordPerfect, AbiWord (free), Pages (Apple), OpenOffice (free - similar to LibreOffice)

Layout: Adobe InDesign, MS Publisher

Graphics: Paint.NET (free), Adobe Photoshop (or it's free Express edition), and several online offerings

---

The Fine Print:

In these sections I'll offer expanded explanations and details about the steps; some side information. You can accomplish everything without reading these at all. But if you have a question, you might find the answer here.

First off, you can do everything with just Word. CreateSpace will give you everything else you need. Why wouldn't you do that?

The word processor is good for writing. It is not designed for layout. The first book I published I used MS Word exclusively, as at first I did not get the hang of using a layout program and being under pressure of a deadline, I fell back on what was familiar. After struggling with section breaks, multiple page headers, etc. I knew that I needed to learn Scribus if I was going to publish another book. Now, over 10 books later, I will only design a book with Scribus. I'll use LibreOffice (since I'm now on Linux) for writing.

Directions

There are 7 steps to creating your own book. (Times are approximate.)

Step 1. Set up formatting styles in your word processor
Time: 30 minutes

Step 2. Write your story!
Time: 30 days to 10 years

Step 3. Prepare your story for layout
Time: 1-3 hours

Step 4. Set up a template in your layout program
Time: 30 minutes

Step 5. Import your story into the layout program
Time: 2-4 hours

Step 6. Add the front pages and Export to PDF
Time: 1 hour

Step 7. Build your cover and Export to PDF
Time: 4-8 hours

Total time (not including step 2): 9-17 hours

The Fine Print:

Each step is explained in its own chapter. The order of steps is not set in stone - you can build your cover first, for instance. Or add your front pages. This is just one way to do it.

However, the biggest step is writing your story. If you haven't written it yet, then all you'll focus on are steps 1 and 2. There are a plethora of great websites and books that can help guide you in writing your story.

If you've already written your story, without the use of styles, then formatting it in your word processor is the first step. In that case, complete step 1, then go through your story and format each paragraph with a style. I know, it will be tedious. But it will be worth the effort. If you choose not to, do not despair. If you use LibreOffice, then when you import the text into Scribus you can replace whatever styles it brings in with the ones you've defined in Scribus. You can do this with Word, too, but only if you save it as an .odt file.

Step 1
Set Up Your Word Processor
Formatting Styles

For fiction, I recommend a minimum of 3 styles for your story:

1. Heading 1 – your chapter heading style

2. First Line Indent – each paragraph indents slightly on the first line

3. First Paragraph of Chapter (optional but common) - the opening paragraph to a chapter does not indent. (Some books also do this at the beginning of each scene after a scene break)

4. Scene break (optional) – allows for proper centering of a scene break on the line (if it's text)

What is a scene break? Have you ever noticed a gap between 2 paragraphs in the middle of a chapter? Or three *'s, or a little graphic? That shows a break between scenes in the story.

Why the scene break style? If you use anything but a blank line, and you center a first line indent, the break will be slightly off center. You can use the first paragraph style and center it, but in either case you're manually adjusting every break. (And when you import to your layout program, you'll lose this information.) Think of each style as being something you can adjust separately throughout your entire document. If you need it, add it.

The Fine Print:

What's the benefit of setting your styles before you write? There are several.

First, when you write, your book will automatically format the way you want it to. You don't have to go back and do a lot of manual updating. If you don't like the look of a style, you can make a slight change and apply it to your entire document. This is a tremendous time saver.

Second, when you publish, the publishing programs expect specific things.

Styles bring consistency without effort. And they're required for proper publishing.

Access the Styles List

In LibreOffice, go to:

> *Format* (Alt-O),
> *Styles and Formatting* (y),
> or press F11 to bring up the Styles and Formatting box.

If you don't see anything, that will be because your styles are docked. You should see an arrow on the right side of your document. (It's a white arrow in a gray vertical bar.) Click it to open the sidebar.

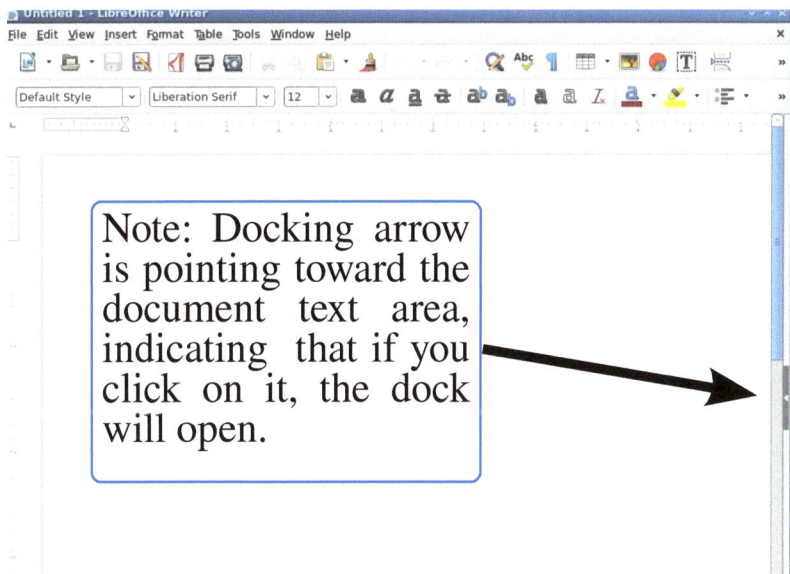

Note: Docking arrow is pointing toward the document text area, indicating that if you click on it, the dock will open.

The Fine Print:

In LibreOffice versions prior to 5 I did not see the sidebar, so opening styles would take you directly to the styles list. After working for a while with the sidebar, I came to find it improved productivity with everything just a click away.

Whatever your preference, you can adapt the program to the way you like to work. This should be true for any software. If you don't already have a commercial product like Word, then get LibreOffice. It's quite capable, and it's free.

Clicking the sidebar arrow opens the sidebar (when it's pointing toward your text). If you've already selected styles and F11, then the styles will come up in the sidebar as shown below.

If you don't see the styles list, click on the green triangle with the T behind it.

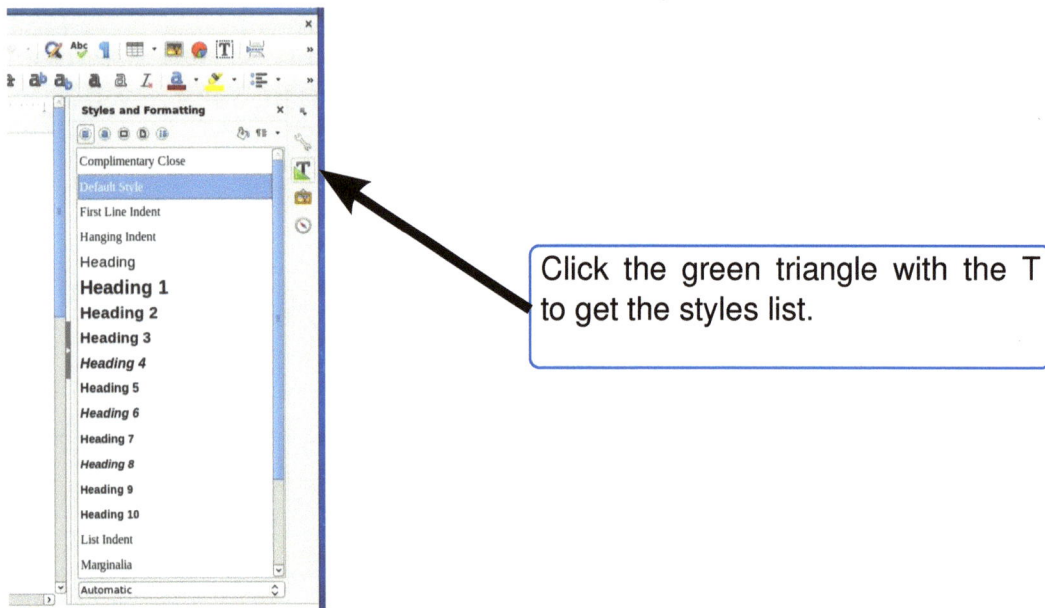

Click the green triangle with the T to get the styles list.

The Fine Print:

Once you've opened the sidebar, clicking on the icon of what's open will close the sidebar, but leave the icons visible.

Clicking the T with the green triangle, with Styles and Formatting open, will close them, but still show the icons so you can click them again to open the sidebar for whatever you need (whether it's Properties, Styles and Formatting, Gallery, or Navigator).

With any software, take the time to see what you can customize so that it works the way you work, or at least closer to the way you work. I'm not a fan of the Microsoft ribbon, so whenever I use a version beyond 2007, I customize the menu and close the ribbon. The few minutes it takes to do this are easily recovered as I regain the productivity I've lost via the ribbon.

You can undock the styles list and move it off your document, keeping it open, if you like. There is a little dropdown menu arrow in the upper right. Selecting this will give the menu shown below left.

The top four choices, from Properties to Navigator, are the four icons along the right side of the sidebar (where the green triangle/T is for Styles, the wrench above it is for Properties). If you put your mouse on each icon (without clicking it) you'll see what the icons are for.

Clicking to undock the sidebar gives you the freedom to move it around on your computer screen and put it where you want to, so that it's readily available, but not in the way of your writing.

An undocked sidebar looks like the below right.

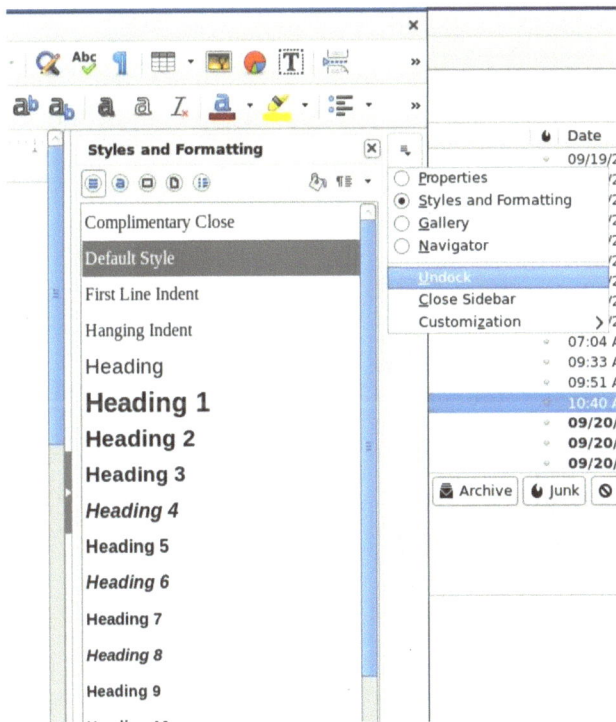

The Sidebar menu in LibreOffice

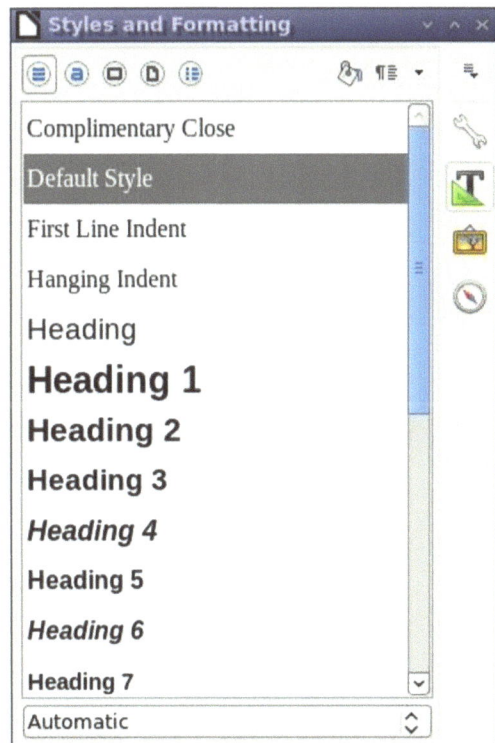

Undocked Sidebar in LibreOffice

You'll see the list of styles already defined. I used to create my own, but didn't see any advantage, so now I just modify the existing ones. If you make up your own, go in reverse order, from main body text up to heading 1. Since we're using the supplied styles, we'll go top down.

Set up the Heading 1 Style

Find Heading 1 in your list, highlight it (left-click on it once), then right-click and choose Modify. (You can do this without left-clicking first as well.) This brings you to that style's dialog. We'll begin from the left side, and cover the tabs that are of greatest interest.

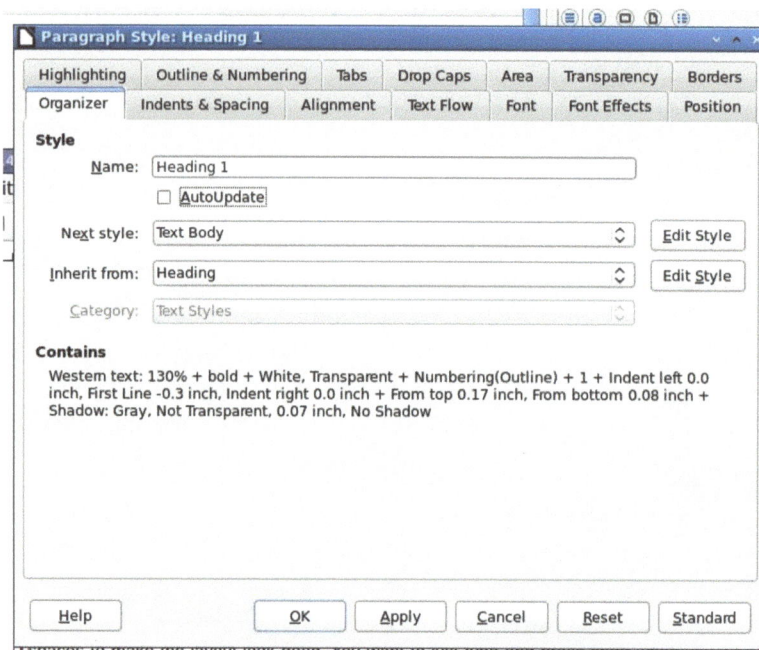

The Organizer tab in LibreOffice 5.0
New tabs in Version 5 include Highlighting, Area, and Transparency. Gone is Background. The tab details we are interested in are unchanged.

The important field on the Organizer tab is Next Style. This indicates what style to use when you press Enter to start a new paragraph. Here we make the decision on what format our first chapter paragraph will be. Block or indented?

Most fiction I've read starts a chapter (and sometimes a scene) with a block paragraph (fully justified). Then succeeding paragraphs have an indent on the first line.

Change Next Style to Text Body.

Select the next tab to the right, **Indents & Spacing**. There are three sections.

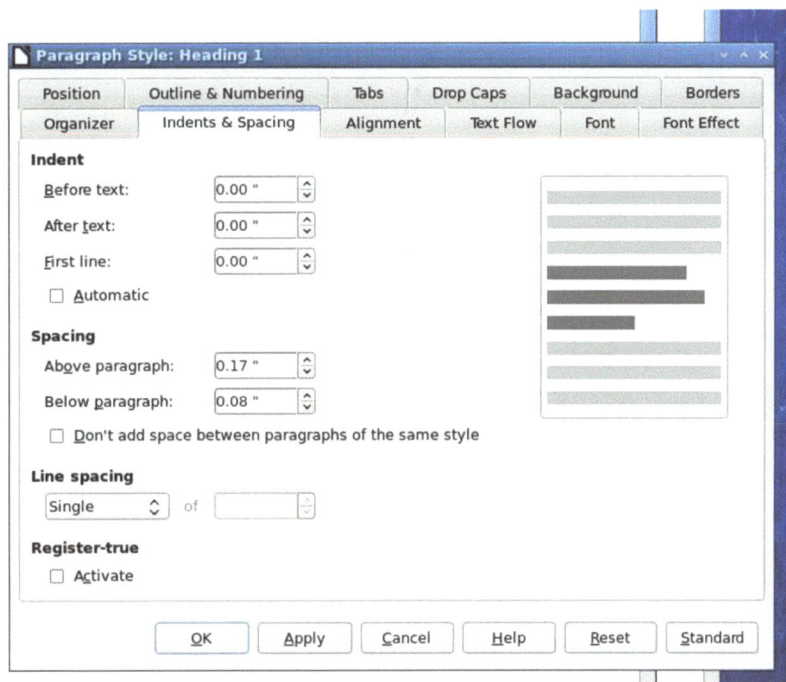

The Indents & Spacing tab in LibreOffice

Zero out the first section, **Indents**, as this is the title. The picture to the right with the gray lines will show you the effect of any number you put in these fields, so feel free to experiment when you get to the body styles.

The second section is **Spacing**. This is more important for your ebook than your print book. Leaving the defaults works fine. (That puts a little space above and below the line.)

Line spacing is the last section we'll look at. I leave that at the default single, but you can choose what you want. Now move another tab to the right.

The Fine Print:

Once you've created all your styles you can save the file as a template so you can use it again without having to go through the process of recreating the styles.

The purpose of styles is to format your text so you're not having to add blank lines and spaces to make the layout look good. You want to just type and press enter when you want to start a new paragraph and have everything line up perfectly.

For the header, the **Alignment** tab's most common choices are Left and Center. Choose the one you want. Leave the rest of the settings at their defaults. Remember, this setting is for your chapter headings.

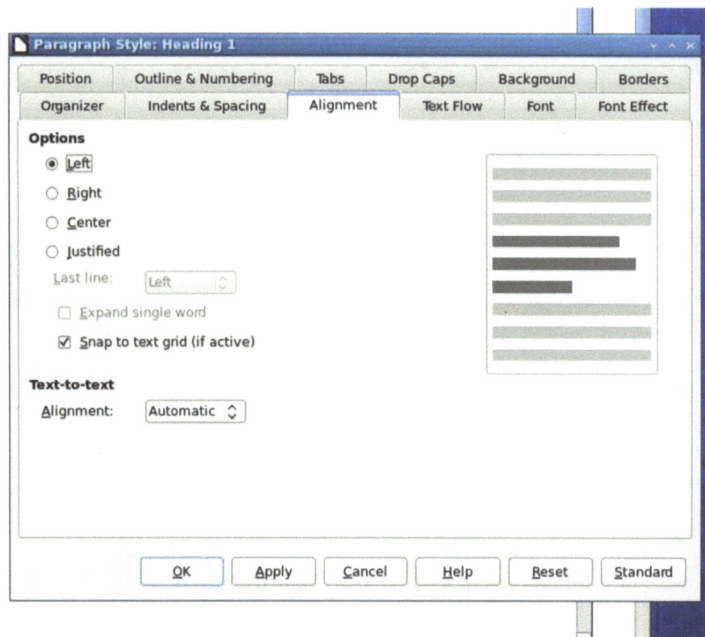

The Alignment tab in LibreOffice

The Fine Print:

You can get fancy with your chapter headings in your print book, but now is not the time nor the place. Since your word processor is only going to provide the input to your layout program, the basics are all you need. And when you convert the file for ebook processing, the simpler the better.

Yes, there are some other options for ebooks, but for fiction or a basic all text (or mostly text) book, don't go overboard with special formatting. It will usually mark you as an amateur.

A good gauge to use is to look at the layout of a book you want to emulate, and duplicate its style.

Self Publish for *FREE*

Finally, we move to the **Font** tab, two tabs to the right. Choose the font you like and what style you want for it. One note of caution: Word processors offer the four styles (regular, bold, italic, bold italic) on every font, whether you have a rendition of the font in that style or not. When you move to Scribus, the layout program, you may find some of these styles missing. Unless your font family includes them, you won't have access to them. You may have to change the font family to get similar effects in print.

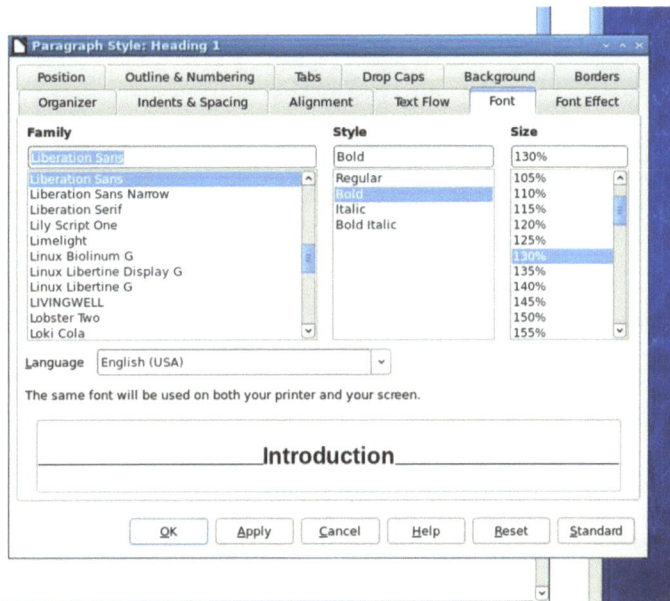

The Font tab in LibreOffice

Size sometimes shows as a percentage. I like to work in fixed sizes. To change it, click in the top field above the selection list (the percentage will match the highlighted value in the list below), and type in the size you want. For instance, type: **16 pt** and press enter for 16 point size.

Click OK to save the changes and move to the next style.

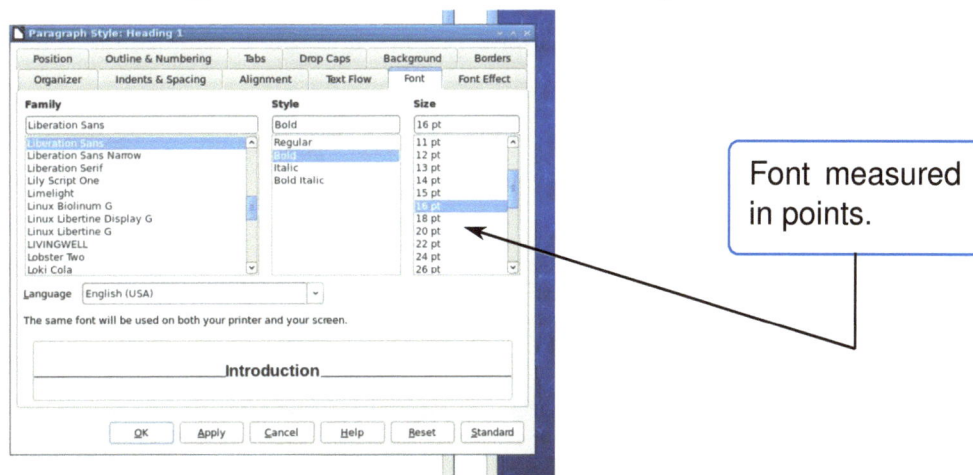

Font measured in points.

Set Up the Text Body and First Line Indent Styles

Block paragraphs and indented paragraphs are similar, so I'll cover them both here, noting the differences.

I'm going to use both styles, so I'll work with the block one first, using Text Body in LibreOffice. I've left my styles list open, but if you haven't, open it up again (Alt-O, y), highlight Text Body, right click, select *Modify*, and on the Organizer tab, select First Line Indent as the Next Style.

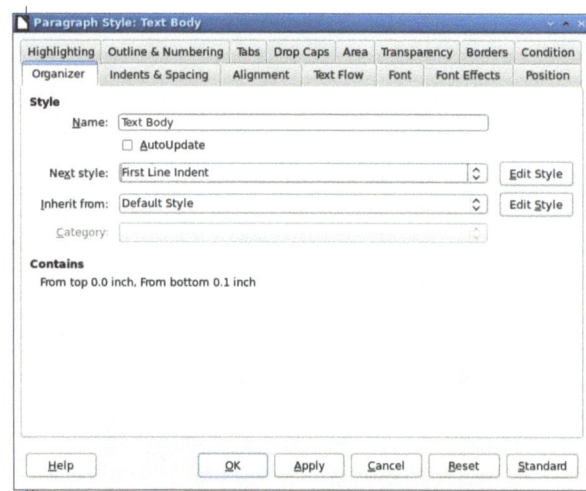

Organizer Tab in LibreOffice 5
Note: You can now edit the Next style from this dialog box by clicking on the Edit Style button to the right of the style name.

The Fine Print:

Now the relationship of the styles begins to take shape. From Heading 1 we go to Text Body. From Text Body we go to First Line Indent. And from First Line Indent, we go to First Line Indent, meaning each following paragraph will be like the one before it, after the first paragraph in a chapter.

If you use scene breaks, then once you create that style, make the next style the one you want for your first paragraph after the break - either block (Text Body) or indented (First Line Indent). Since those styles are already defined, the text will flow just the way you want.

You control the look of your book. And you can do it before writing a single word!

On the Indents & Spacing tab zero out the Indent section fields. In Spacing, zero out above paragraph, and set the below paragraph to 0.10 inch (if it's not already there). This adds a little spacing between paragraphs without having to press enter for a blank line.

Line spacing defaults to 120%, which makes the text easier to read. If you want to save pages, set this to single spacing by selecting from the drop down list in the box where you see the word Proportional.

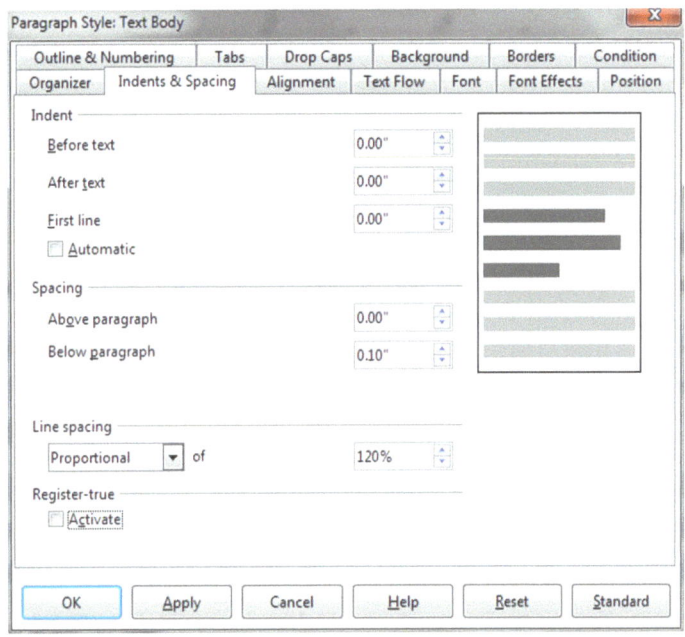

On the Alignment tab choose Justified, and leave the Last line field at Left. What this means is that if the last line of your paragraph is short, it won't be expanded to meet the right margin, with the inherent large spaces between words.

Choose the font you want to use on the Font tab. Set the size to 12 pt.

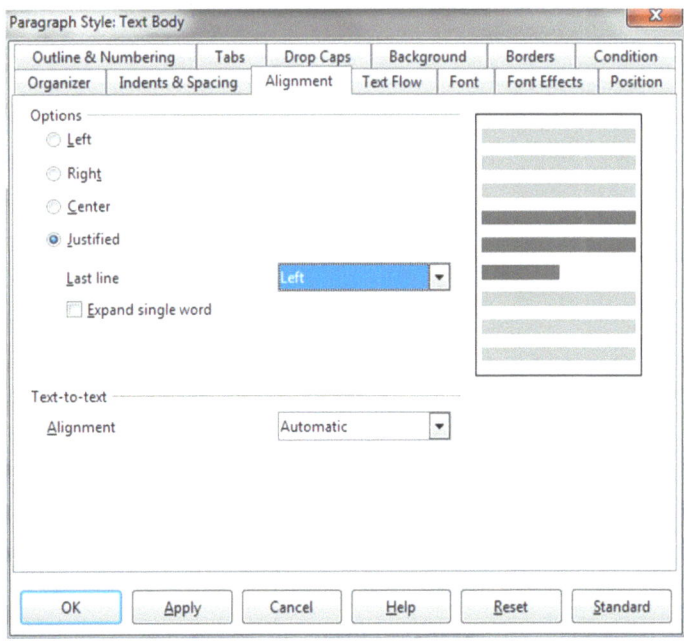

Repeat the above for your First Line Indent style. On the organizer, the Next Style should be the same, First Line Indent, so that as you build the paragraphs they will all have the same style after the opening one in the chapter. The only difference between this style and the Text Body style is the indent.

You'll notice the first line is set to indent 0.20 inch (if not, set it to that value). You can see by the picture how it looks. Everything else should match the settings you used for your Text Body block paragraph style, since it's all part of the same area of the document.

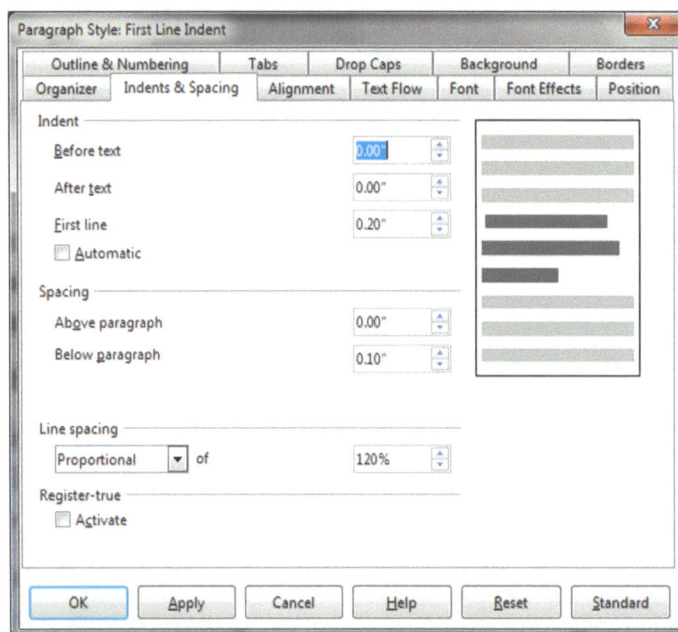

The Fine Print:

The default tab width in Word is .5 inch. If you leave this as is your printed book will look odd. Again, the proof is in looking at published books. Take a ruler and measure the indent. You'll see it's typically a quarter inch or less.

It's these little details that will add polish and a professional look to your book. For an ebook it's not as important, as readers can adjust fonts and layout based on what they are reading the ebook with - a proprietary reader, a web app, etc.

As in many other endeavors, the more time you spend up front preparing, the less time it will take you in the end to produce that published book. I've been able to complete the layout for a 200 page book in less than 4 hours when I've set everything up first.

Optional: A Special Style

There's another style you might want to create, and that is one for scene breaks. Why a different style? When I put together my first book, I centered my scene breaks using the First Line Indent as the base style, and just modifying it in Scribus to center that line.

Not only did this require manually adjusting each scene break line, but when I looked at the break, it wasn't really centered. It was a little closer to the inside of the book due to the beginning indentation. Is that a big deal? No. But if you want it to look the best, I'd suggest creating a new style just for scene breaks.

The advantage of using a separate style is that you don't have to keep centering all the breaks (if you use only two defined paragraph styles). I call mine SceneBreak.

Select Text Body, right-click, and select *New*. This will begin a new style based on your Text Body style.

Below left: Type in the name of your style and select the next style.

Below right: Using Text Body, we only need to adjust the alignment, to center the scene break.

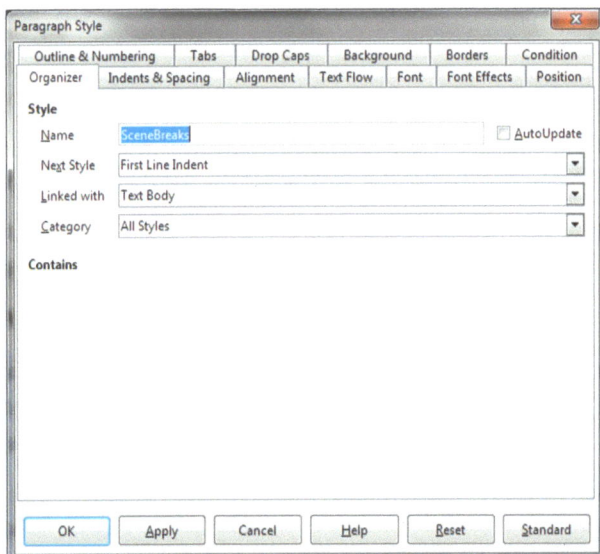

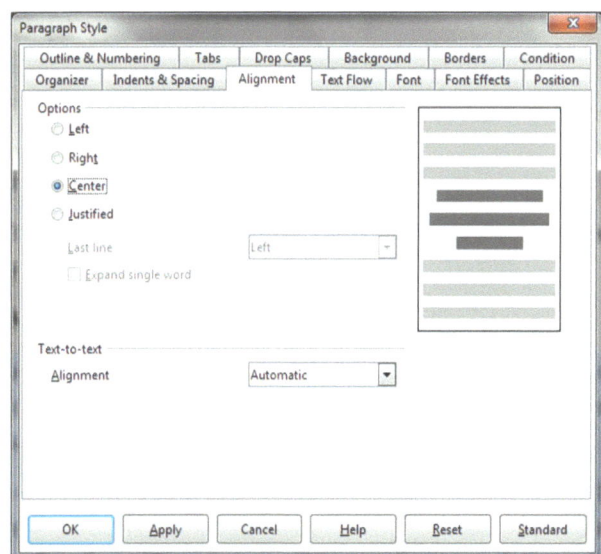

Step 1 is complete! And that didn't take long, did it? I'm guessing you've already begun writing your story, or even finished it. In that case you'll have to go through your manuscript and add or update all the styles. Most word processors will set all paragraphs to the default style. Sounds like a lot of work, doesn't it?

Is there a trick to making it fast and easy? Yes! Highlight your entire document and select the First Line Indent style. This will handle most of your text. All you have to do now is go from chapter to chapter (and to scene, possibly) and reformat with the other styles (Heading 1, Text Body, SceneBreak).

Let's recap.

Set up at least 3 styles:

Heading 1 – required (almost) for ebook formatting – makes table of contents easy to do.

Text Body – the first paragraph after the title, and possibly for the beginning of each scene, no indentation, full justification. (I used to call this Block Para, until I realized for the writing portion it was unimportant. I give them more descriptive names in the layout program.)

First Line Indent – every other paragraph, where the first line begins in slightly (not half an inch!).

SceneBreak – copied from Text Body but centered, so the scene marks will center on the printed page. If you're using graphics for your scene breaks, this one is not required.

When the body of your story is finished, you'll want to add the front pages. For ebooks you may add a couple pages, but that's usually it, and you can just format those on the fly, or use a couple of the other Heading styles (like 2 and 3) to set your title size and name size. The key is not to use Heading 1, as this is used for your table of contents when using some ebook formats.

The Fine Print:

Ebook in a flash! Can't wait to get your ebook out there, ahead of your print edition? Don't want to skip pages to find the ebook section? Familiar enough with your software?

Bookmark each chapter (Heading 1 style). Go back to the front, add a page before chapter 1, and add your table of contents. Link to each bookmark. Add 2 pages in front, the first for your title, subtitle, and name. (Apply your special styles to these.)

On the second page, put your copyright information, a short acknowledgement section, (remember, your readers want to read the story!), ISBN if known, publisher (CreateSpace if using their ISBN). Save it, then save as html (Web Page, Filtered, in Word). Then upload!

Step 2
Write!

You've now completed Step 1, Setting up your Word Processor Styles. Now it's time to begin step 2, the longest step in the process. You have to write your masterpiece.

If you've already written it, or are in the process of writing it, you can modify your document using the previous chapter on styles, so that as you continue or go into revision mode, you'll be prepared for the layout step. So don't despair if you've already written 50 or 100 pages. It will take some time, but not a lot, to add the styles to each paragraph and chapter heading.

There are many books and websites devoted to showing you how to write the best story you can, and so I won't attempt to offer any advice here. Nor will I send you to any specific websites, though you can find some on our website, at www.soulattitudepress.com.

Since everyone's style of writing is different, I won't promote one over another.

Use the style that's most comfortable for you.

The Fine Print:

I'm not going to kid you, this is the hardest step of them all. It will take the longest time. Just keep your eyes on the goal, whether it's a book for family and friends, a business manual, or that great novel you hope will become a bestseller.

In the end, you'll be amazed and excited to hold your work in your hands. And if you give it to family as a gift, it will be something they will cherish - a gift from your heart.

So, what are you waiting for? Get writing!

Step 3
Prepare Your Story for Layout

What? you ask, screaming in disbelief. Isn't that what we covered in Step 1?

No. It's not. If your writing is complete, it's very close to becoming an ebook. A table of contents, the front title and copyright pages, and a cover and you're done.

But for a print book, in order to build it quickly, there is another step in the process. It's optional, but I found it saves a lot of time.

Separate each chapter of the book into a separate file.

How? I copy the story as many times as I have chapters. Then I open each one, remove all the chapters that I don't want, and re-save it with just one chapter in each file.

This way my styles remain consistent within each file. The purpose of doing it this way is to speed up the import of the text to our layout program, Scribus, with as little adjusting as necessary once the text is brought in. We'll see this in action in the coming steps.

The Fine Print:

What's important here is to hold off adding the front pages, called the front matter. If you do, you'll just have to strip it from each file you create when splitting the book up. In addition, the front matter for a print book is typically different from an ebook. We'll cover the front matter at the back of the book.

By copying the file and splitting it, you won't lose your styles. You can also save the styles in a template, which is helpful when you're ready to start writing your next book. For this exercise, though, that's unimportant. We'll focus on getting the first book out.

Now that your file is split by chapter, it's time to tackle the layout program. Fear not!

Step 4
Set Up a Template in Your Layout Program

Prologue: Why Use a Layout Program

Scribus, the open source layout program, is what we are using to format our book for print publication. There are several benefits to taking the time to set up the template. One, if you are writing more than one book in the same format, then you only do this work once. Two, if part way through the process you want to start over, again, you have the template complete and can just begin a new file to import your story.

Think of a layout program as a scrapbook. In a scrapbook, you paste in pictures and things any way you want, organizing them with complete freedom.

That's basically what Scribus does for your story. You play with the pieces and lay them out the way you want them to look. For a fiction or a mostly text memoir, this is relatively simple.

Why use a layout program? CreateSpace accepts documents in other formats (.doc, .docx, .rtf). Some people offer templates for Word to make it easier to format your book. Should you feel more comfortable doing that, then by all means, invest in those templates.

For me, the reason to use a layout program is a simple one: Control. You have complete control over the layout. The first book I published I formatted in MS Word. It had about 30 different running headers (sections), and poetry on every page. It took days to get it right. With Scribus, it would have only taken hours.

The Fine Print:

LibreOffice saves by default to .odt format. (Open Document Text) The interaction between an Open Document Text file and Scribus is different than with a .doc or .docx file, and reduces the amount of work involved in laying out the book. If you use Word, your last step should be to save as an .odt file.

If you use Word, before getting ready for Scribus, save your file as an Open Document Text (.odt) file, making sure all your styles transferred correctly. You can still use the Word file for your ebook.

If you don't have Word, LibreOffice makes an excellent choice as a substitute.

Settings For the Template

The template is where you describe the dimensions of your book.

Before loading the text, we want to define all the parameters that Scribus needs in order to produce the book to our dimensions. For a fiction book, popular sizes include 5x8 (5 inches wide by 8 inches high), 5.5x8.5, and 6x9. I like the 5x8 size for paperback fiction under 300 pages, but I've seen many books in the other two sizes as well, with 6x9 probably being the most popular.

If you are going to use CreateSpace, this would be a good time to download their directions for margins. (We'll cover them here as well, but it helps to understand what they are looking for at a minimum.)

The parameters can be split into two categories, the second category being specific to the software.

General parameters: (you can decide these ahead of time and write them down)

> Size of your book

> Margins – inside, outside and top and bottom

Scribus specific parameters:

> Automatic text frames (every new page adds a text box for you)

> Formatting Styles (similar to your word processor)

> Master pages (one key advantage to a layout program)

The Fine Print:

It's a good idea to write down the settings, even though it may seem tedious at first. The reason for this becomes clear when you copy and paste one section to another, and then have to line it up. Knowing the margin dimensions for each left and right page makes it easy to reset the text frame if you're not using automatic frames. And even if you are, because sometimes you just have to do something you didn't expect to do.

What are master pages? They allow you to set what you want to show on every left-facing page and right-facing page. They allow you to define how a page with your chapter heading looks, if you want it different from the others. They are wonderful timesavers!

When you first open Scribus you are presented with the Document Setup dialog. Spend some time just looking at it to become familiar with the 4 sections. (3 parts Document Layout, 1 part Options)

The tabs across the top handle file creation and opening.

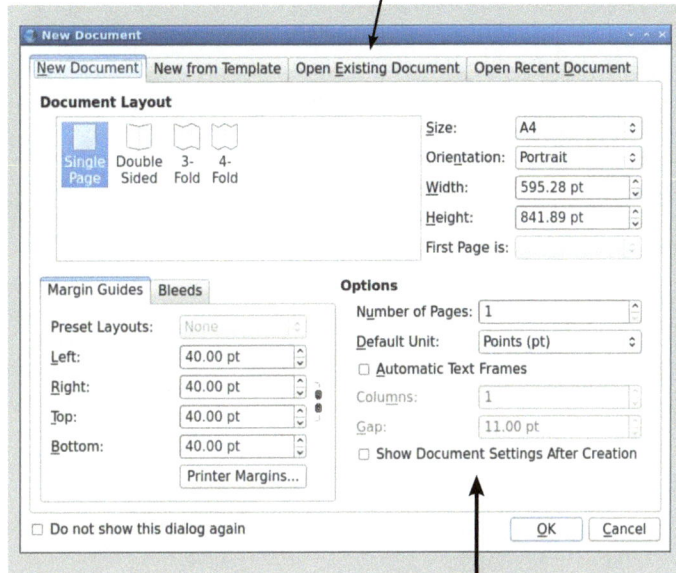

Page size settings

How Scribus behaves.

The Fine Print:

My first thought in looking at this page is, what are points? So I change the Default Unit to inches. Now, clockwise from upper left, click Double Sided for Document Layout.

For size, click the drop down and choose Custom, and then you can put in the width and height of your book. The first page is which side faces you when you open the book.

Options handle how Scribus acts. You can set the number of pages Scribus creates when you click OK. Scribus saves faster with fewer pages, so no need to add a bunch of blanks until you need them.

If you check Automatic Text Frames, then every time you add a page to the end it will add the default sized text frame.

Finally, the margins and bleed. We won't use bleeds, so we'll just set the margins from what we decided earlier. [Bleed indicates the area images extend beyond the margin.]

For CreateSpace, we'll fill the Document Layout section this way:

Click on the double-sided graphic.

Size – Custom, Orientation – Portrait, Width and Height your dimensions. Note: Under options I've chosen inches as my default measurement.

First Page is – Right Page.

Margin guides: Set your margins as you have chosen, inside, outside, top and bottom. For fiction without graphics, we won't set bleeds.

Number of pages – We'll choose 100 as a starting point. It will take a little longer to set up and save your document. But we're only talking seconds.

Automatic Text Frames – check this box and Scribus will automatically put a text frame on each page, using the margins you've chosen.

I set my top margin .25 more, because I'm going to add a header. If you want a footer, add the .25 to the bottom margin. Inside margin also gets an extra 1/4 inch (.25) to keep text away from the binding.

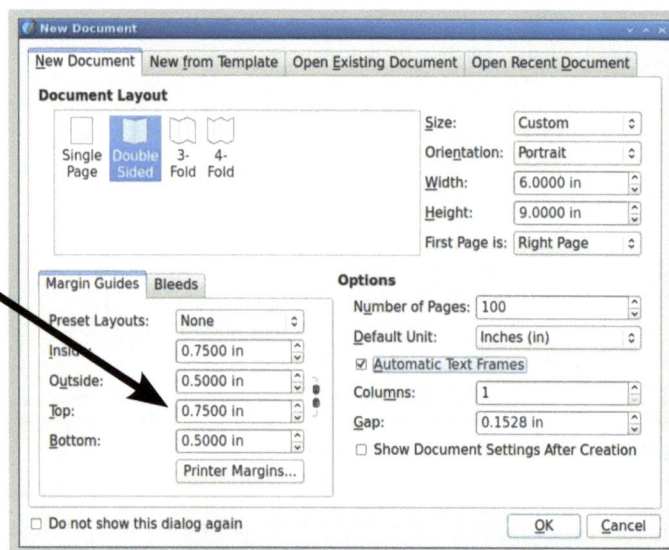

The Fine Print:

Now I've contradicted myself. Instead of starting small, I put the page count at 100. Why? I've decided it's faster than continually adding blocks of pages. And for fiction, it's all text.

But just starting out, you may feel more comfortable with a small page count until you get comfortable with the program. (You can always add another 100 very easily.) I've done it both ways, starting with a small set of pages and adding each time I insert a new chapter.

How you choose to do it is up to you. And if you're writing a memoir and want a series of pictures, say, in the middle of the book, it might be easier to only start with the page count you think will get you to that section of your book. We'll cover why later.

Formatting Styles:

Let's set up our styles first, before we move on to the master pages.

Our first style will be our chapter header. This will match our Heading 1 style in LibreOffice. Press F3 to open the Style Manager. You'll see the default styles that come with Scribus. Not many.

So let's get started!

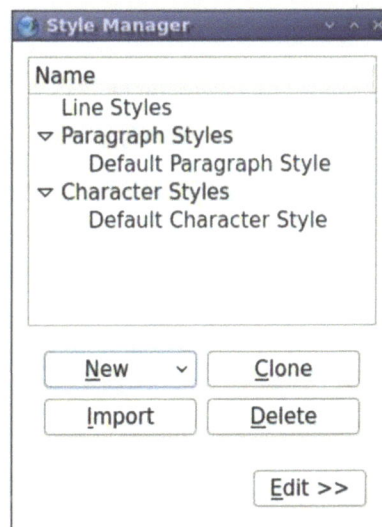

The Fine Print:

We'll create styles to match our document. We can do that using the New and Clone buttons. The Import button is for importing from another Scribus document, so once you've created styles, it's easy to reuse them.

I like to name mine so that they group together. So all my paragraph styles start with 'Para', my chapter headings 'Chapter', and so on.

Though the dialog boxes are different, the settings are similar between Scribus and your word processor style options.

The Styles box is free floating, so you can keep it open and move it where you want at any time.

Adding a Style

We'll add our first style by highlighting the default paragraph style and clicking on the Clone button. We are presented with a Properties tab, to manage the style properties, and a Character Style tab to set up our font.

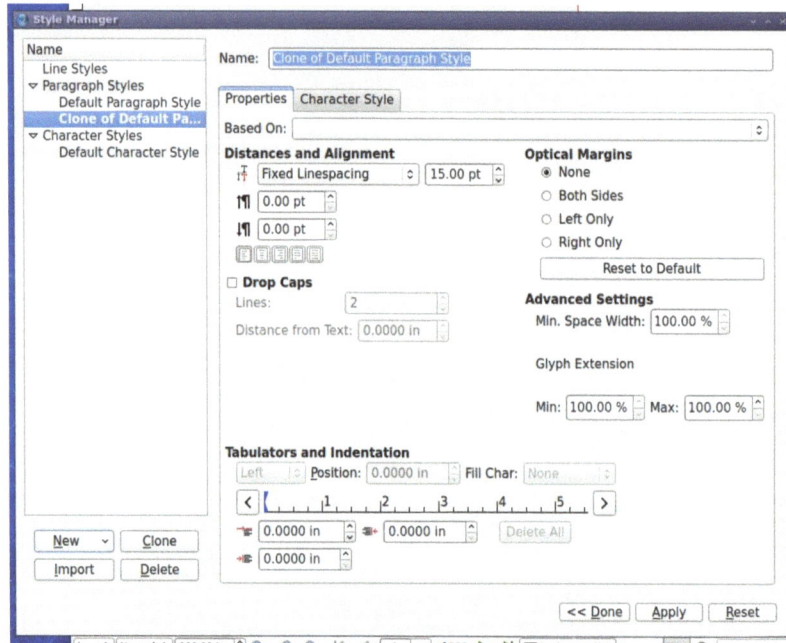

The Fine Print:

We'll only cover the settings we need, and ignore the rest. Feel free to investigate them on your own.

On the Properties tab we're only interested in the Distances and Alignment section and the Tabulators and Indentations section. We're going to set our alignment (center, fully justified), and our indents (for our first line indent style, for instance).

On the Character Style tab we'll be interested in the font style and size.

We'll build our **ChapterHeader** style first.

Here are the steps we'll take:

1. Type the name of your style in the top box: ChapterHeader

We're on the Properties tab, and we'll focus on alignment, since this style is really just for 1 or 2 lines, depending on how you write your chapter headings.

2. Click on the 2nd icon from the left of the alignment icons just above the Drop Caps check box. This is the one for Centered. (They are, from left to right: Left, Center, Right, Full Justified with last line left, and Full Justified.)

Now click on the Character Style tab. We'll focus on the Basic Formatting section, and leave the rest of it alone.

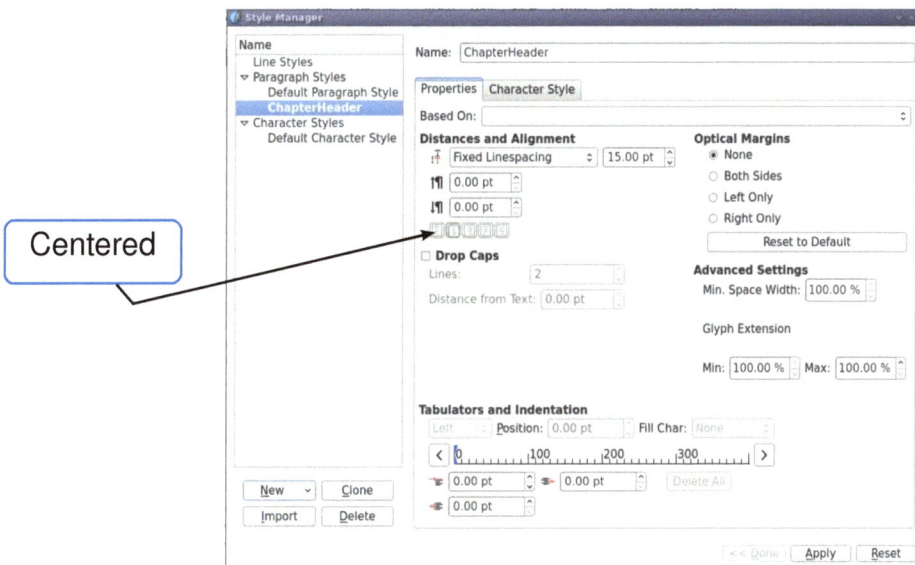

Centered

The Fine Print:

Here's a trick to getting this done a little faster.

Once you complete your style definition, click Apply to create it, then click Clone on the left to copy it to another style. (Or highlight the style you want to copy and click Clone.) This way you don't close this dialog box, saving a step.

Also, clone from the style most like the one you're creating, and you'll have fewer changes to make.

3. Family – this is the font family. Depending on which one you select, you'll have the option of one or more styles. This is where you'll see a disconnect between Scribus and your word processor. Scribus does not make up styles. It can only use those that were specifically created. (Your word processor can mimic other styles programmatically.)

I like a bold font for my chapter header, though with larger sizes, or the right type of font, this may not matter. Scribus won't show you what they look like. What I do is set up a font page in LibreOffice to choose which fonts I will use so I can picture them prior to printing.

In his first book, author J G Michaels used a spelled out chapter number. In his second, he used numerals in a wood-cut style font. Since he liked the look of that, we'll go with numerals again. The font used is Blue Highway Linocut, and the size is 72 pt. This font only has two styles, regular and italic.

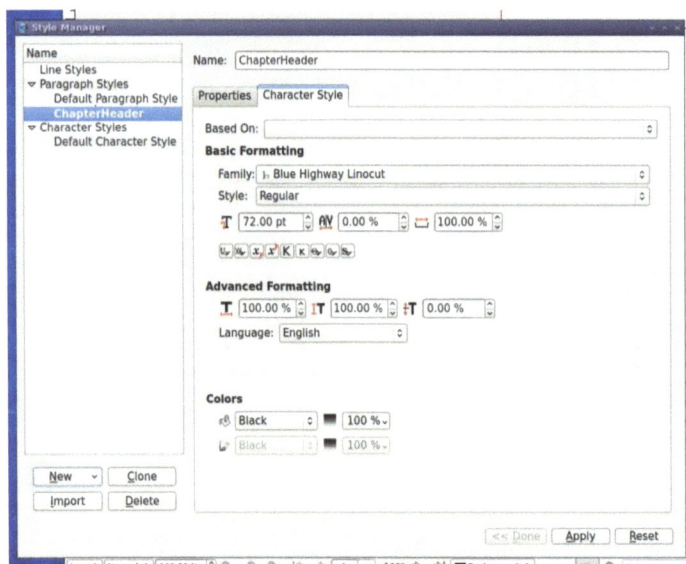

The Fine Print:

In our example, the book being assembled is a compilation of several short stories. Michaels used a different header for each story, separate from the chapters. We called it the Episode Header.

So we'll repeat the above for the Episode Header, in half the size, since we'll be writing the title of each episode. Scribus automatically saves each one as you create it. (The Done button is grayed out.) Click Clone on the ChapterHeader style, change the font size and you're done.

The Paragraph Styles

Now let's set up the paragraph styles that match the Text Body and First Line Indent styles. We start by cloning the default paragraph style and create our BlockPara style (the Text Body). This one's simple, we name it and click the 4th icon above the Drop Caps (Justified with last line left). On the Character Style tab we select our font, Liberation Serif, and accept all other defaults.

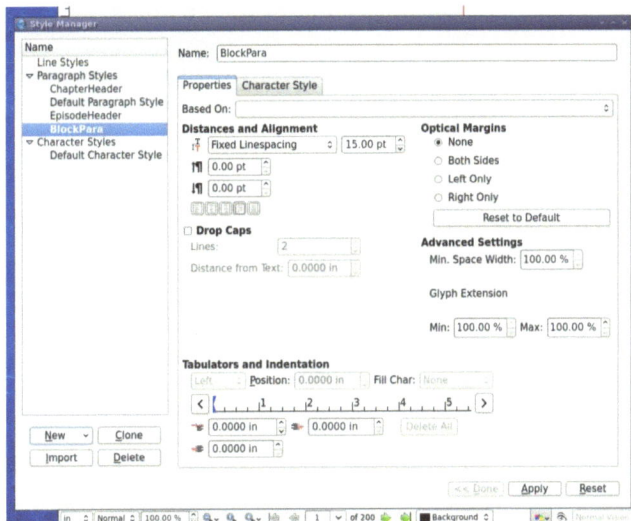

The Properties Tab

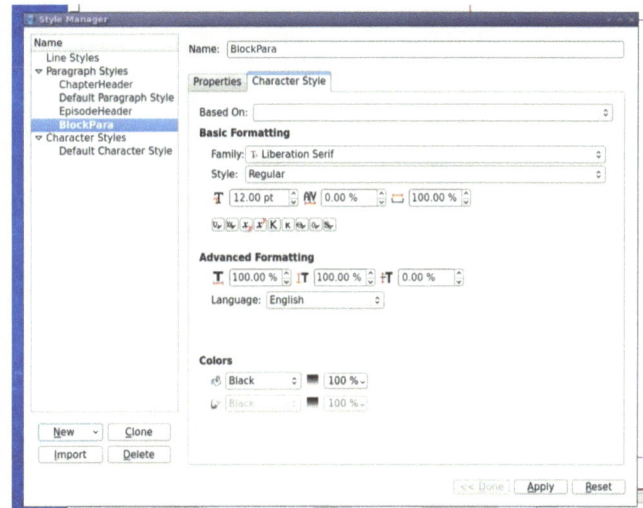

The Character Style Tab

The Fine Print:

Once again, a contradiction! The style name is reversed. Why? Well, it's up to you how you want to name them. In this case, I chose the name as I would say it, rather than how I might group it.

There's no right or wrong way, only the way that you like to do it. With this contradiction, I show you that you have options.

Notice it's not easy to tell which alignment you've selected. It grays the background of the icon, but it's difficult to see.

Now we clone this style for our First Line Indent and name it. The only change is at the bottom of the Properties tab, we change the indent to .2 on the first line, in the Tabulators and Indentation section.

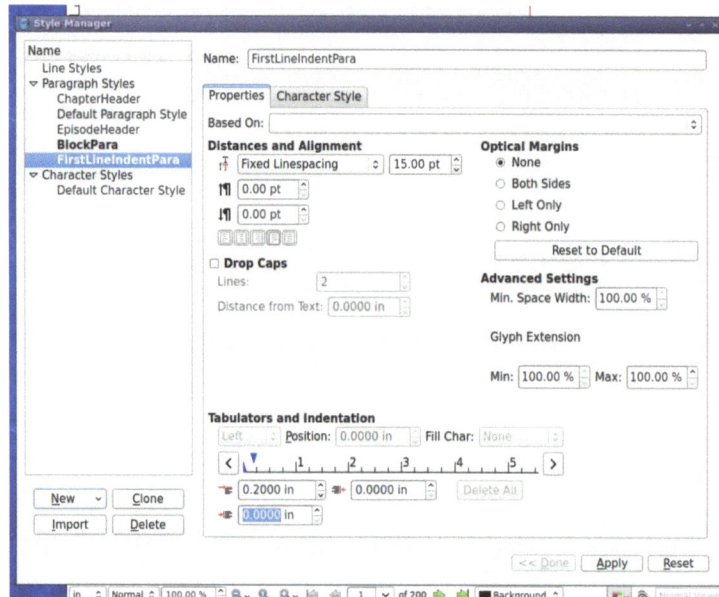

We'll also set up the scene break style, cloning BlockPara to SceneBreak, with the only change being the alignment on the Properties tab. We'll choose Centered.

The Fine Print:

And now you see how easy it is to copy a style and modify it, if you use a similar style to base it on.

Another option for naming styles is to make each one start with a unique letter. That way, if you need to change a style and you get the dropdown list, all you have to do is type the first letter and it selects the style you want. This will come in handy later when we're replacing styles after we import our text.

Special Styles

Now we come to the special styles. You can create as many of these as you want, but I find I need a minimum of four: the running header style, left page number and right page number styles, and the copyright page style.

For the running header, I prefer a size that's slightly smaller, so I'll choose 10 pt. Instead of 12. I like italics to set it apart from the body. I'll use this for the page numbering also, but need two new styles because I want the page numbers flush against the outside margin. Therefore, the right page will be right justified and the left page number will be left justified. I clone my RunningHeader and adjust the alignment to get these 2 styles.

Are the page number styles necessary? Not really. When you define your master pages you can justify the page number manually the first time, and it will propagate to each page correctly. This is how I did it before, but I'm thinking ahead now, because if I want to use this template again, that's one less action I have to take.

For the copyright page, I want it left justified. You could use the Default Paragraph Style, but I like to name mine so I know where they are used. I'll set the copyright text at 11 pt.

Here's the final list.

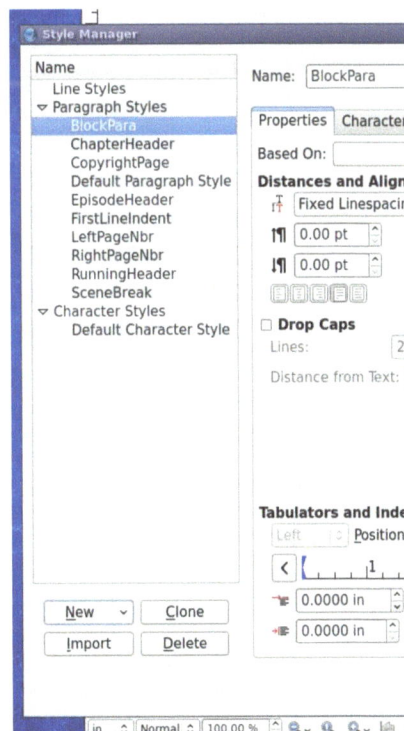

Setting Up Master Pages

Master pages are helpful for setting the page numbers automatically without having to add them to each page as you go. Scribus starts with two, a left and a right. You can modify these to include your headers. These pages will include a running header, and the page number.

Before you set up your master pages it's helpful to know the dimensions of your left and right page text frames. To find the measurements, press F2 to pull up the Properties dialog, and select your first text frame (Text1), which is on the first page (right).

Write down the X and Y positions, and the Width and Height. Repeat the process on the text frame on page 2. These are your right and left settings.

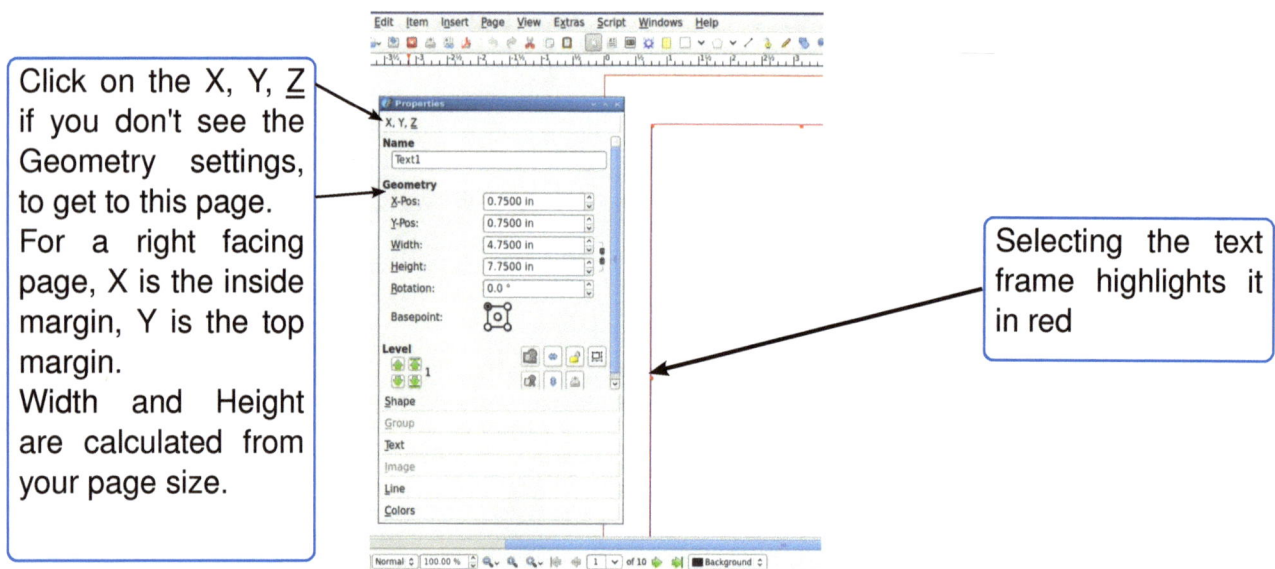

Click on the X, Y, Z if you don't see the Geometry settings, to get to this page.

For a right facing page, X is the inside margin, Y is the top margin.

Width and Height are calculated from your page size.

Selecting the text frame highlights it in red

The Fine Print:

Having these dimensions handy will help if you delete a text frame and want to replace it with one of the same size. If you add pages to the front of the document, it won't add text frames automatically. You can copy and paste a text frame, or just create a new one using your saved dimensions if desired. Save both left and right page Geometry settings.

Tip: Always insert pages in pairs if they aren't at the end of the document. This preserves the proper page alignment.

Now you're ready to begin.

On the first page of your document, select Edit from the top menu (Alt-e), then Master Pages (M), near the bottom of the list. It comes with 2 defaults. I use these to copy to named ones.

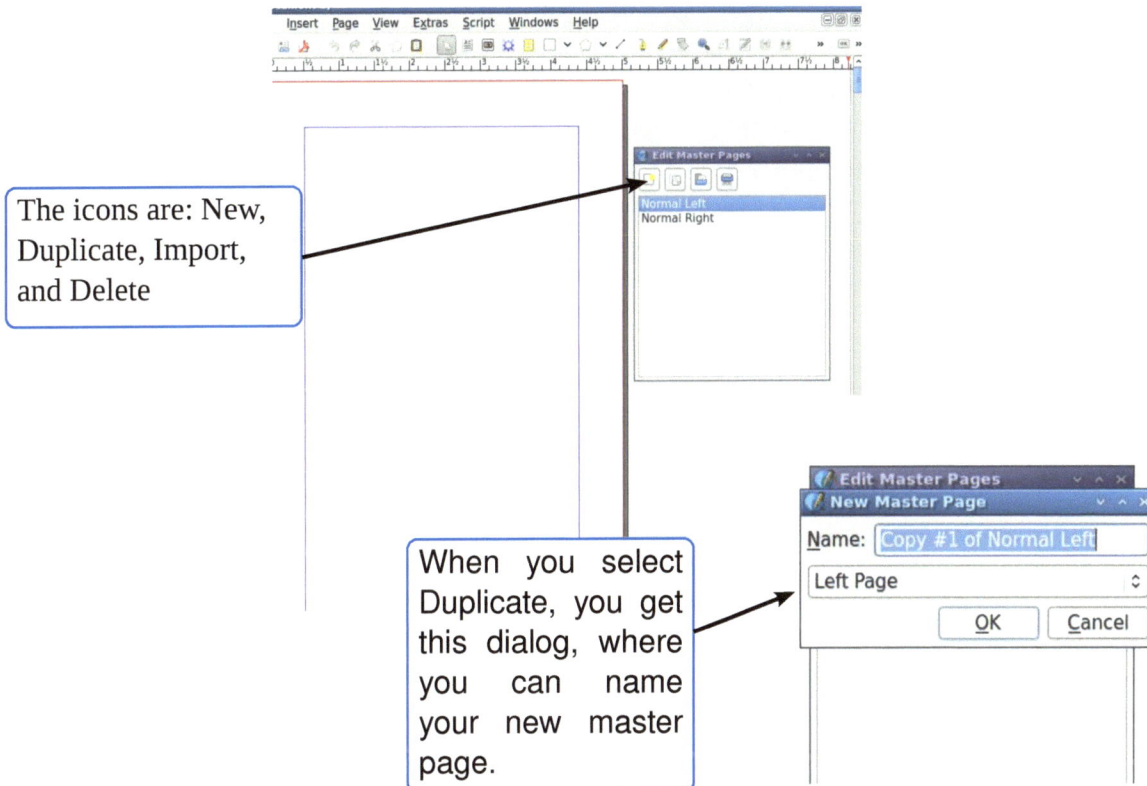

The icons are: New, Duplicate, Import, and Delete

When you select Duplicate, you get this dialog, where you can name your new master page.

The Fine Print:

That's right. You can import Master Pages you created in another document. Another timesaver. You only have to do this once if your next book will look the same as this one.

Tip: I number the master pages in the order I want to see them for selection purposes. Like: 1 Numbered Left, 1 Numbered Right, 2 Chapter Left, etc. The pages are listed in alphabetical order.

Chapter pages typically don't have page numbers or headers/footers. You can use them for the front matter pages as well.

The page you are looking at now is your left master page (Normal Left). Click on the right master page (Normal Right) and you'll see the page change, where the larger inside margin now shifts to the other side. (The blue box designates the margins you set up in the beginning.)

Okay, let's set up the left page first. This is your even numbered page (because page 1 begins on the right).

First we'll add a small text box above our top margin (because we have room that is printable). Select *Insert, Insert Text Frame*, or just press the letter t on your keyboard. You'll see the cursor change into a plus sign with a little page icon, and X and Y values. Click and hold the left mouse button and drag to make a rectangle.

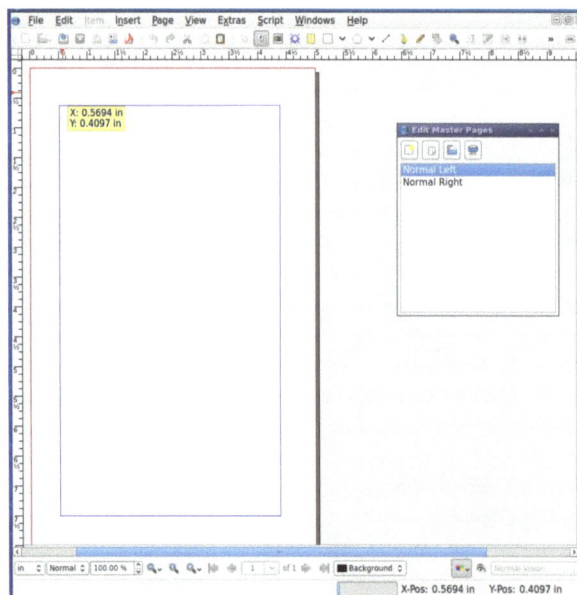

The Fine Print:

We're demonstrating putting headers on your pages. Some authors prefer page numbers on the bottom, and the same process would be used, you would just be working at the bottom of the page rather than the top.

If you do choose to put your numbers and titles on the bottom, increase your bottom margin by .25 inch in your initial setup and use that quarter inch for your numbers and titles. And you can reduce your top margin by the same quarter inch.

There are many ways to fill these headers/footers. Take a look at a book you like (same genre or type of story as yours) and feel free to emulate its layout.

What you want to do is create this thin text frame to be the width of your body text frame. (The blue box shows you the margins.) Then when you center in the header, it will be centered over your content.

Just draw a box, don't worry about if it lines up or not. That's what we'll do with the values we saved from the margins.

Let's set the Geometry values based on our left facing page. We use the same values for X-Pos, Y-Pos, and Width that we wrote down earlier. The only difference will be the Height, which we'll set at .25.

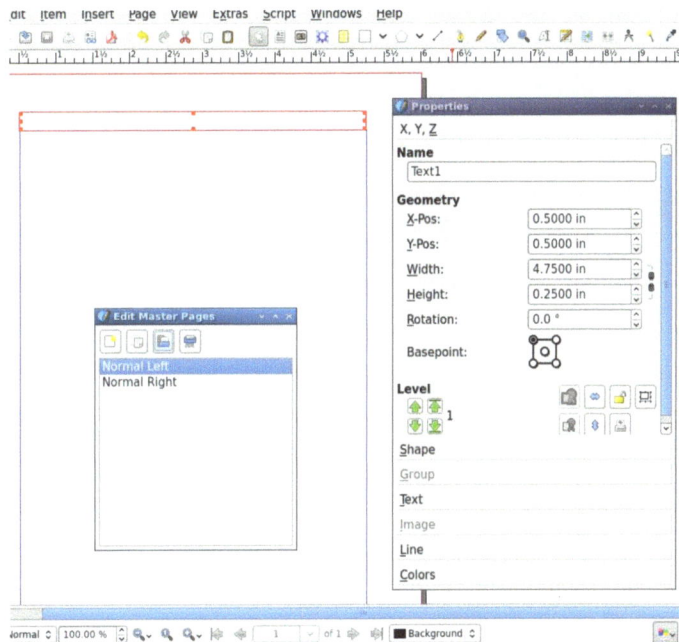

The Fine Print

Another nice use of information we've saved. Notice how the red header text box lines up with the page margins?

Now we'll add the text we want to display on every left numbered page. And we'll add a page number as well, in a separate text box.

For the page number box, create a small text box on the left corner and make it .3 wide (to accomodate 3 digit page numbers).

Now select your text box and open the story editor. It's the little notepad icon up on the right past the big letter A. Or press Ctrl-T.

I typed in the author's name. When you type something, No Style shows up on the left. If you click on it, it gives you a menu showing No Style. Click on that and select the style you want to apply.

We'll choose PageHeader, which is slightly smaller in size and uses italics.

> We'll add a separate text box for the page number. We set the width to .3 inch, which easily handles 3 digits at 11 point size. Notice the author's name centered on the page header.

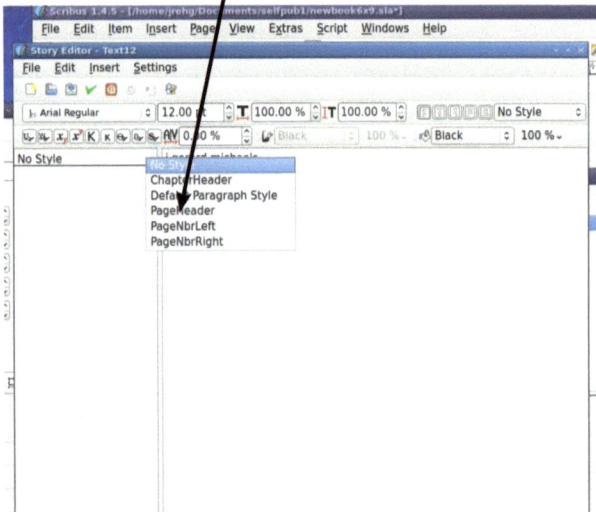

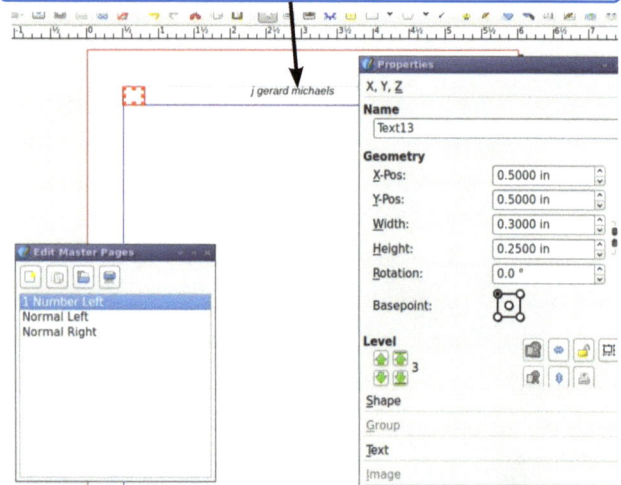

The Fine Print

These instructions work whether you are adding headers or footers. Look at several books similar to yours to see how other authors use this area of the page. You'll find quite a diversity of presentations.

Once you've completed the left numbered master page, do the right numbered master page. You'll apply these pages to any ones that you want numbered.

For chapter heading pages, where you typically don't put numbers, copy the default left and right master pages to new ones. Why do this? I find it easy to choose when I'm applying one to see Chapter vs. Numbered. It's a simple reminder.

Now, let's finish that page number box.

The page number is a special character. Open the story editor (Select the text box and press Ctrl-T or the story editor icon).

Select Insert from the menu (or press Alt-I), and select Character. You'll see a list of categories of what you can insert. We'll choose Character, and then from the list, Page Number.

You'll see a red # (pound sign). I selected a style next, called PageNbrLeft, because on the left side I want the number left justified. On the right hand page, I want it right justified, so that the page number always lines up with the margin, no matter which side it's on.

To close the master page editor, just click on the x in the top right corner.

Now, save the document as a template, so you can use it again. Select File, Save as Template, select a directory, and name your template file.

Then select File, Save As, and create a name for your book file.

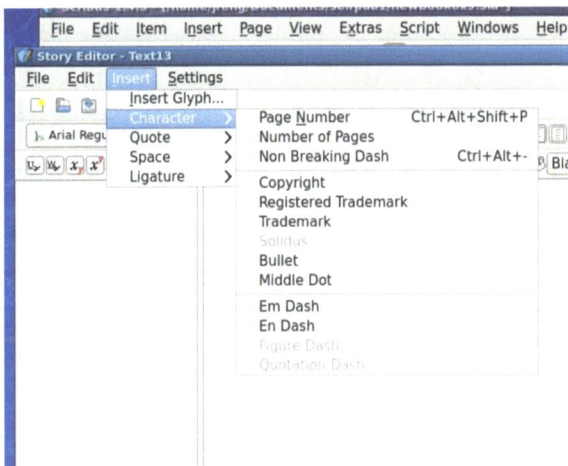

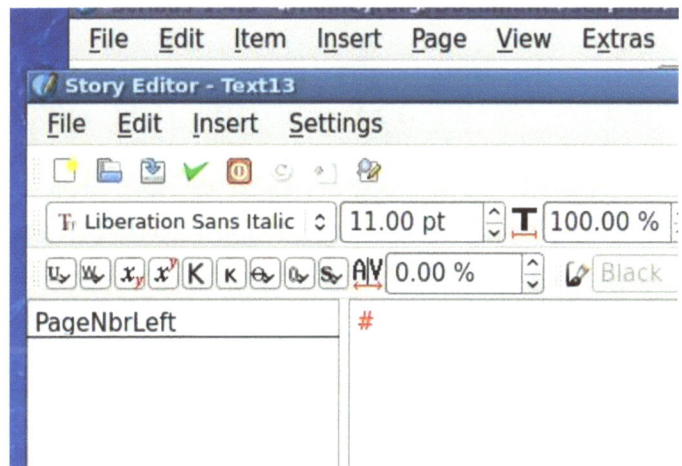

The Fine Print

Congratulations! Once you've completed setup of your master pages, it's time to build your book.

Here's a look at the list of master pages I've created. The Chapter ones are just duplicates of the default ones. You can create as many as you like, but remember, the more you have, the more complicated it will be to apply them.

Now, let's build that book!

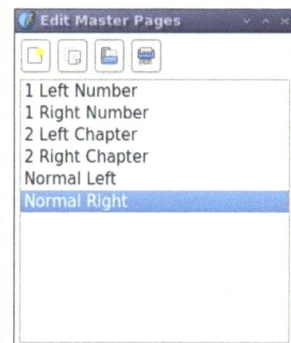

Step 5
Import Your Story into the Layout Program

This is the part you've been waiting for, planning for, preparing for. The step where your story takes shape as a printed book. Here's what should already be complete:

- Your story is formatted properly (Step 1)
- Your story is written (Step 2)
- Your story document is split into separate files by chapter (Step 3)
- Your Scribus setup is complete (Step 4)

I typically begin my file naming process with a number to keep track of versions of the book. So the first file I've saved in Scribus might be called MyStory-1. If I get so far on a given day, then when I begin adding more on the next day, I start by saving it as MyStory-2. That way I can always back up to a previous version if I've messed something up. Also, when you're working on the book, if you make a mistake, select *Edit* from the menu and the first item will be an undo of what you did last. You can remove the mistake this way as well.

The Fine Print

A word about software quality. No matter what software you use, sooner or later you'll run into a bug, or something that will cause it to stop working. Maybe it's a conflict with another program, not enough RAM, whatever. I've had that happen with the most expensive software and the cheapest. If this happens, don't panic!

Close the program and re-open it. That usually clears the problem and you can continue working. If that doesn't work, try a reboot. That's the importance of saving often, and saving different versions. Maybe one each time you add a new chapter or two (when considering Scribus or your word processor).

And for your own mistakes? The Undo option can be a real booksaver!

Importing a File

Let's import our first file now.

You should know which file you're going to import.

- Go to your first blank page and click inside the box, selecting the text frame (Figure 1).
- Right click and select Get Text (Figure 2).
- Choose the file you want to import. We'll start with chapter 1 (Figure 3).
- The chapter is now imported (Figure 4).

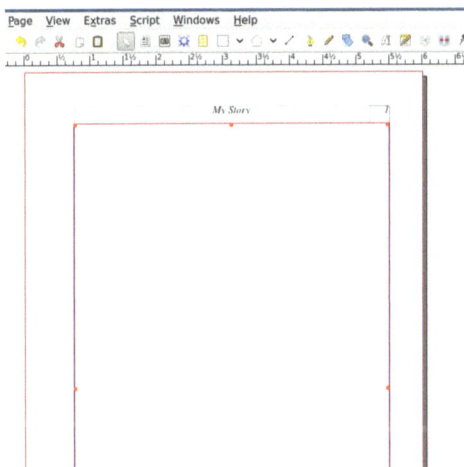

Figure 1

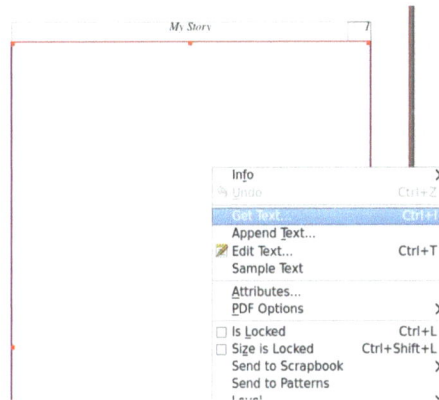

Figure 2

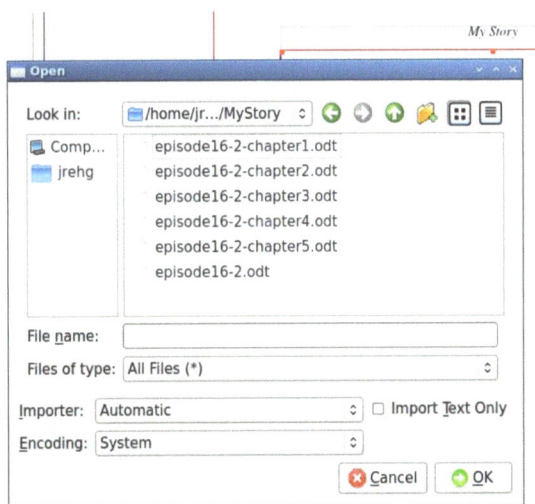

Figure 3

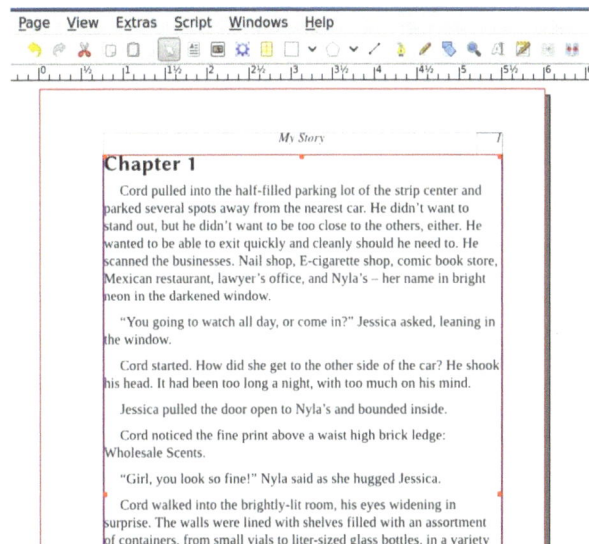

Figure 4

Replacing the Styles

Now that you have the text in Scribus, you'll replace the imported styles with the ones you've created. Open the story editor for the text. (Ctrl-T) You'll see the names Scribus came up with from the .odt file. This will give you an idea of what to replace them with, when it's not obvious.

If the style manager isn't open, press F3 to open it. You'll see the list of all the styles, the ones you've defined, plus the ones created on the import.

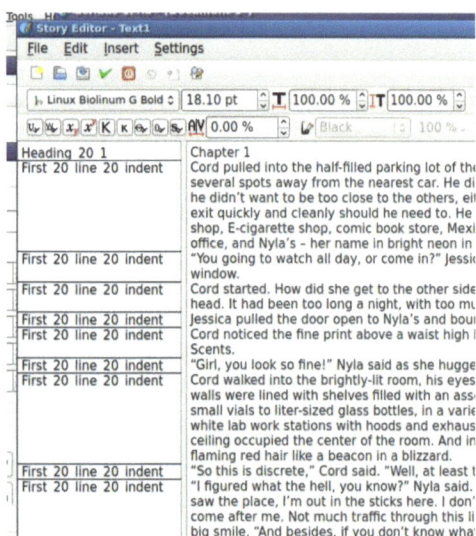

Styles linked to the imported text

Styles after Import

The Fine Print

You may ask, "Why not just wait until everything is imported before changing the styles?"

When you change styles, and add blank lines where you want them, you're changing the length of your import text. It may span an extra page, which would throw everything off. Inserting a single page between pre-defined ones throws every succeeding master page off, making for tedious work to re-align all the pages. My rule? Always add pages in pairs.

What could be different about the styles? For an ebook, the reader can change font size, so you'll typically have 2 fonts, maybe a 12 and a 14. For a print book, you might decide on an 18 or 24 size for your chapter header, and want to space the chapter title down the page 4 or 5 lines. Doing this after you've imported the next chapter invites disaster.

To replace a style, select it and click the Delete button. Then select the style you want to replace it with, click OK, and click the Apply button.

Repeat until all imported styles are replaced.

We'll replace Heading_20_1 with ChapterHeading, First_20_line_20_indent with ParaIndent, and P80 with SceneBreak.

Then we'll add spacing around our chapter header, and replace the first paragraph with ParaBlock style. The end results are below right. By deleting and replacing, we get back to just the styles we defined in Scribus.

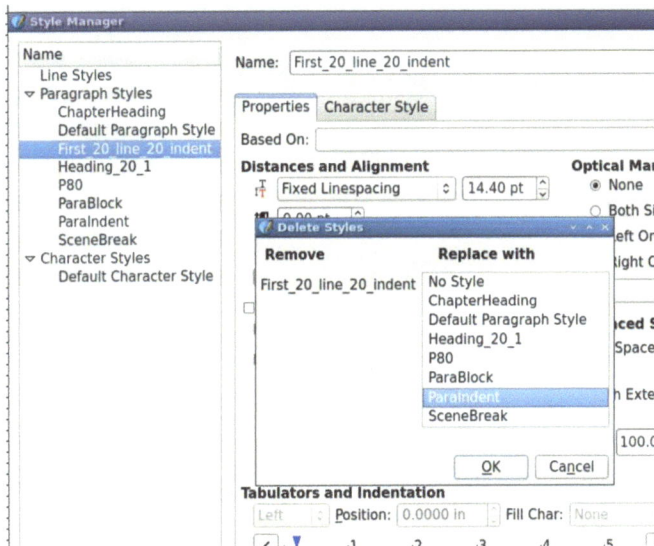

Replacing an Imported Style

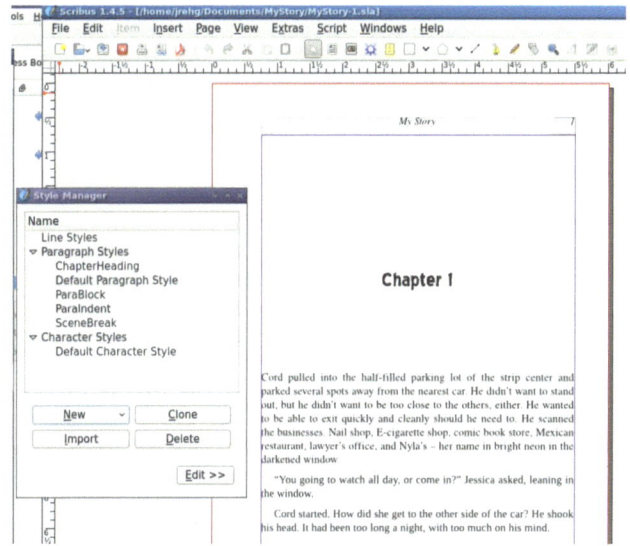

The End Result

The Fine Print

We have just one or two more steps to go on the chapter. Then, we'll just keep repeating the same process, over and over.

Be aware that the styles imported may change names. One reason for this is if you have a blank line in your text document, it will assign a style to that as well, which may throw off how it names the other styles. It's important to open the story editor each time to verify what styles will replace the imported ones.

The imported styles have a "_20_" in place of each space in the style name.

Now, let's look at some of the issues that may come up, and how to handle them.

End of Chapter Adjustments

Once you've finished with the style replacements and your chapter spacing, go to the end of the chapter. Think of it this way: You have one long ribbon of text, and it may extend beyond a single page, covering as many as are necessary. We check the end to see if we have enough pages in the book to display the chapter. You can see it at the end. If there's not enough, Scribus displays a small red x in a box of the last text frame.

When you run out of pages, and you will unless you overestimate the total, you'll need to add more pages at the end. These added pages will automatically include text frames.

The Fine Print

Like other software, there's more than one way to do the job, and Scribus is no different. You can start with 500 pages and delete the ones at the end that you don't want, or start with 10 and add 10 at a time. It's up to you. There are trade-offs with each method; choose the one that best fits the way you work.

You'll load and save faster by starting with fewer pages, but have to add more when you run out. Let's add some extra pages, then we'll take care of the last thing before we add another chapter.

We need to add more pages so we can see the rest of our chapter. To do that, select Page, Insert, from the top menu and fill out the dialog box as follows:

- Put in the number of pages you want to add.
- We're adding them 'At End' so we leave that as is.
- For the master pages select your numbered ones for left and right.
- Click OK.

The outcome is shown below right.

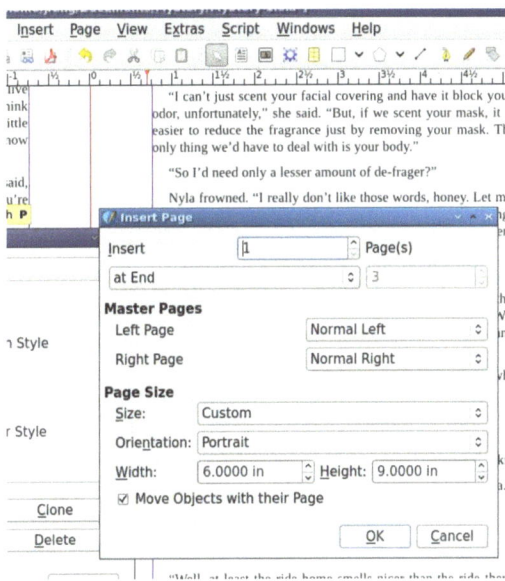

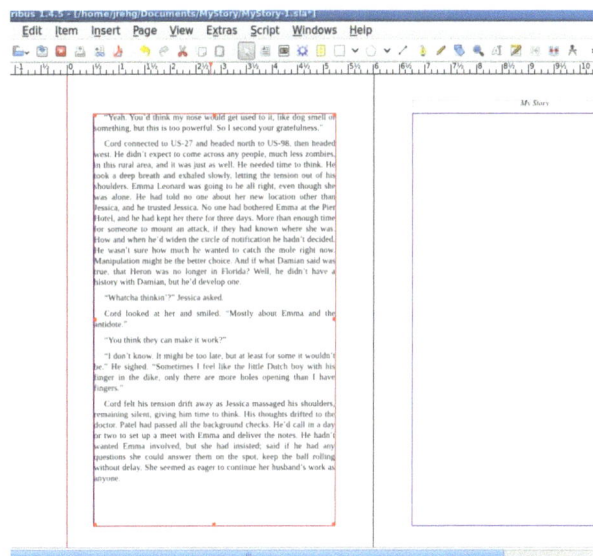

The Fine Print

You've added 10 or 20 pages and they are all numbered master pages. But you know that some of them will be chapter pages. What to do?

You can apply a master page to any given page, at any time. Or even an entire series of pages. We'll take a look at that when we are ready to import the next chapter of our book.

Once you get comfortable with the steps to add a chapter of your story to Scribus, you'll find yourself getting more efficient at it. As long as you save often, feel free to experiment. There's so much you can do, and we're only touching the basics here.

Now that you have enough pages to extend beyond your text, you're almost ready to add the next chapter. There's just one more step to take.

You'll have to unlink your last filled text frame from your next empty one. Unlink? What's that? Just for the fun of it, click on the first empty text frame and open the story editor. What do you see? Did it surprise you?

It's your previous text. Why? Because you're still looking at one ribbon of text, unbroken. In order to start a new section, or chapter, you have to disconnect from the previous one. This is called unlinking.

With your last text frame selected (that has text showing), click on the Unlink Text Frames icon (Or press U) to see what frames are linked together.

Then click on the text frame you want to unlink, in this case, the empty one.

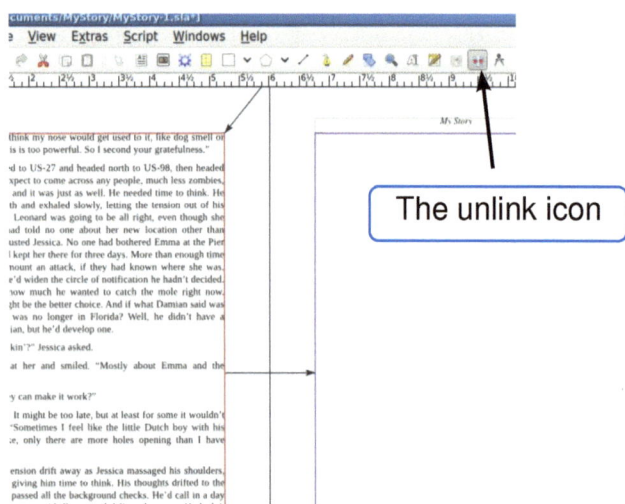

The unlink icon

The text frame above is linked to 2 others, the one on the page before, and the empty one on the next page. (Noted by the 2 arrows.)

Selecting the text filled frame and clicking Unlink verifies that the empty frame is unlinked. The connecting arrow is gone.

Now apply your chapter master page to the blank page.

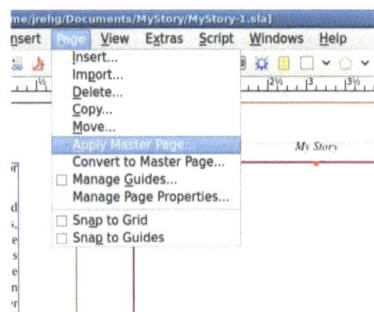

Click Page, Apply
Master Page

Select the Master
Page and click OK.

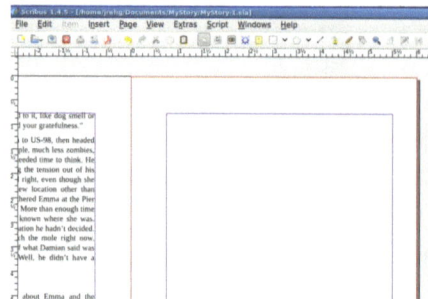

The end result. No header.

Import Recap

Let's recap the steps it took to import our first chapter. (If you have a prologue, that would be your first file to import.)

Select your text frame and get the file to import:

Right click, Get Text, select your file

Replace the imported styles with your styles:

Review the names, delete and replace

Go to the end of the chapter and If necessary, add more pages:

Page, Insert, enter page count and master pages to use

Unlink your last filled text frame from your next blank one

Select frame with text, press U, select next empty frame

Save, then repeat until all your files are loaded into Scribus!

The Fine Print

Scribus Keyboard Shortcuts: (case doesn't matter, T is the T key only)

Ctrl-T - open the story editor on the selected frame (Edit Text)
U - unlink a text frame from the selected one
F3 - opens (or closes) the Style Manager
F2 - opens (or closes) the Properties dialog
Ctrl-S - save the file

Others that you may end up using that come in handy:
(Some will be discussed in the pages that follow)

T - Adds a new text frame
I - (not L) - Adds an image frame
N - link a text frame to the selected one (if you unlinked by mistake)

Step 6
Add the Front Pages and Export to PDF

There are 6 front pages to add, but again, this is not a rule that's set in stone. Look at books similar to yours and adjust as you see fit. This is the scheme I like to use:

Page 1: The title

Page 2: Blank

Page 3: The title, author's name, and publisher's name

Page 4: Copyright notices, ISBN number (if you have one)

Page 5: Dedication, Acknowledgements, or Foreword page

Page 6: Blank (or continuation of page 5)

The key to remember is that you want to add pairs of pages, not an odd number. Otherwise it will throw off all the following pages' alignment.

Once you've completed these pages, then it's just a matter of exporting to PDF so you can upload your document to CreateSpace.

The Fine Print

Before you add your front pages you might consider adding more styles. One for your title, one for your name on the title page, another for your publisher name, and one for the copyright page. By doing that, if you don't like the size and composition of the front pages you just have to edit the styles to see the changes. You don't have to go back into the story editor in each text frame.

It's tempting to just manage the limited amount of text on these pages manually, and that's okay, too. There are many options when it comes to using the software; feel free to explore and find the way it works best for you.

Go to the first page of your document, and this time, when you select Page, Insert, and type in the number 6 (if that's how many pages you're putting up front), change the box that says At End to Before Page. You can leave the right and left pages at the default, or choose the master chapter pages as I show here.

Make sure this says *before Page* so they are added to the front.

Note it defaults to the page you are on, so you can actually do this from anywhere in the document, as long as you set it to before Page 1.

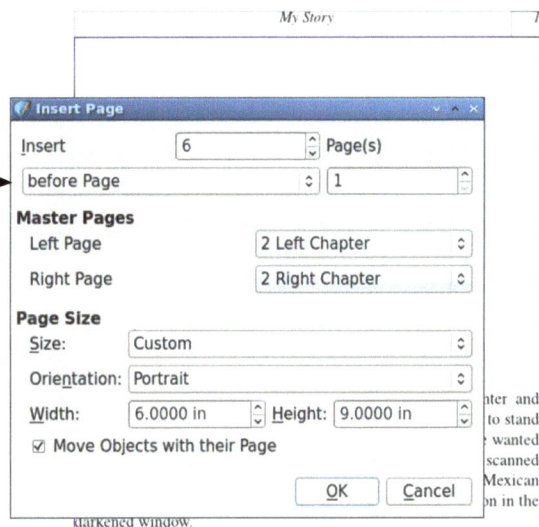

Insert Page

| Insert | 6 | Page(s) |
| before Page | | 1 |

Master Pages
Left Page: 2 Left Chapter
Right Page: 2 Right Chapter

Page Size
Size: Custom
Orientation: Portrait
Width: 6.0000 in   Height: 9.0000 in
☑ Move Objects with their Page

OK   Cancel

The Fine Print

When you insert pages at the beginning, it won't add the text frames automatically, even if you selected that on setup. That's not a big deal, as these pages aren't typically filled with a lot of text, so we can put in frames of any size we choose.

Once again, it's helpful to write down several of the position settings so you can duplicate the frame on another page. For instance, you can copy the page from 1 to 3 and be part way done with some of the work.

However, you don't have to copy the settings if you don't want to - you can always copy them right from the Properties dialog. (F2)

Page 1

Press T (Insert, Insert Text Frame from the menu) to insert a text frame on the first page, and drag it to any size shape. Then take a look at your saved text frame width and make it that wide so that when you center text, it will be centered on the page.

I like to use half the page, centered, and place the title slightly above center.

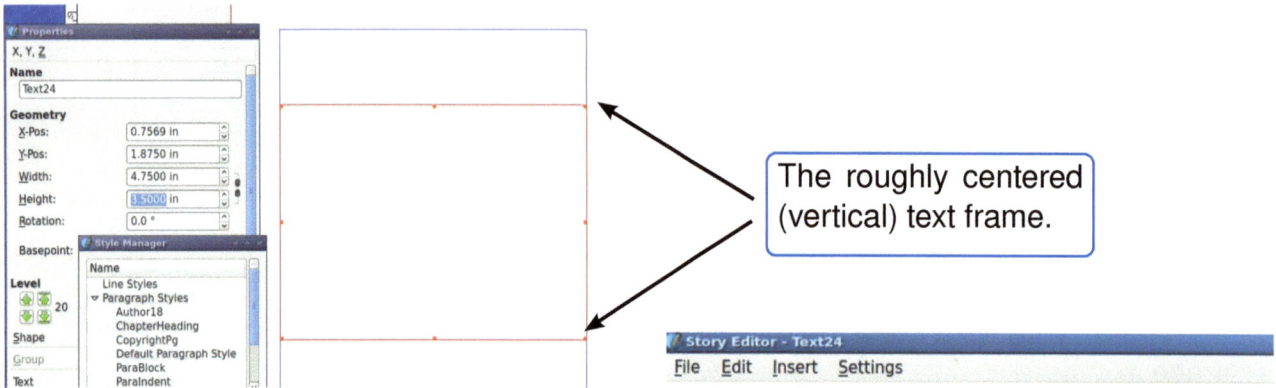

The roughly centered (vertical) text frame.

In the story editor I space down several lines before I add text. If you select a style first, and then press enter, the style should repeat on the next line. If it doesn't (this doesn't always work), put your cursor back at the end of the above line and press enter again.

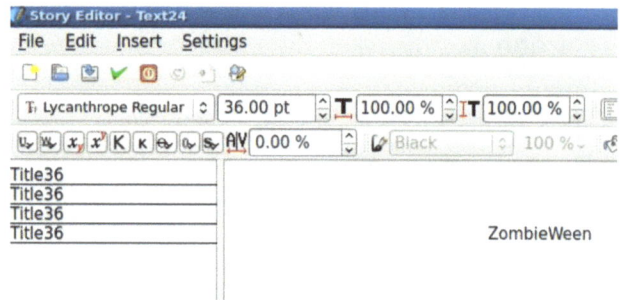

Check your alignment and add/remove blank lines as you see fit.

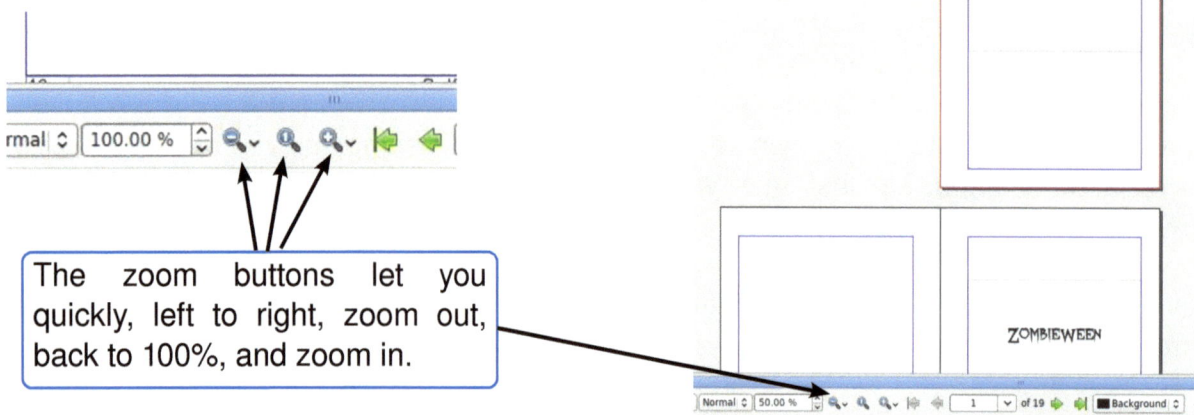

The zoom buttons let you quickly, left to right, zoom out, back to 100%, and zoom in.

Page 3

Page 3 adds information to page 1, so we can copy and paste our text frame and add the missing pieces. Just as in any other program, Ctrl-C copies and Ctrl-V pastes.

Select your text frame (click inside so the frame turns red) and press Ctrl-C to copy it.

Move to page three and click on the empty page. Then press Ctrl-V.

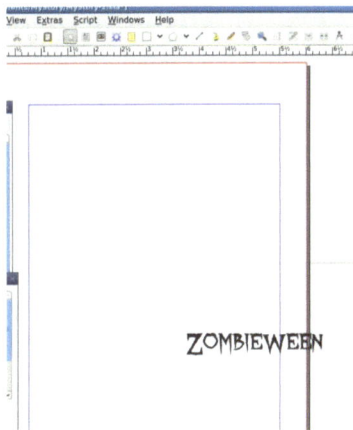

The Paste drops the frame outside our margins

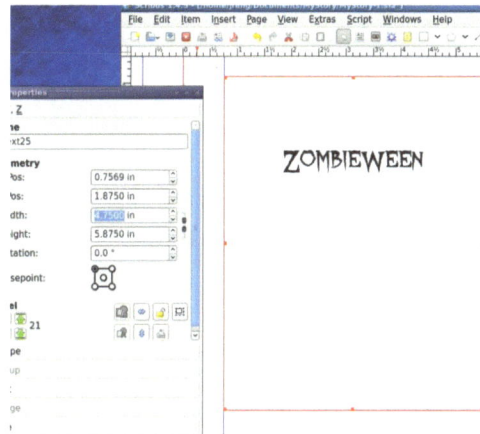

We can copy the X-Pos and Width or type it in based on Page 1.
F2 opens Properties if it's not visible.

The Fine Print

The rest of the front pages follow a similar pattern. If you need to use the entire page, set a text frame with the same X, Y, Z properties of a regular page. Then play around with blank lines in the story editor until you get the text on the page looking the way you want it to look.

You can move the text frame around with your mouse, but if you want it to exactly line up with other frames on other pages, the position settings are the most accurate. (Under Geometry on the X, Y, Z tab of the Properties dialog.

If it doesn't fit exactly right, you can also edit your style to affect a change to the page, reducing its size, changing its font. With separate styles for the front pages you're confident it won't change anything else inside your book.

Export to PDF

Congratulations! If you've made it this far, you now have a completed interior book! All you need to do is put it in the proper format and upload it, create a cover and upload it, and you've got a book published!

We'll export your file as a pdf. Select File, Export as PDF. You can also click the script A icon (save as PDF) on the menu bar (under the Insert menu item).

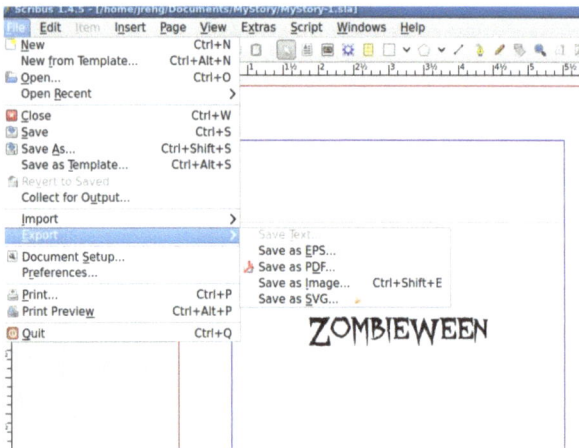

Scribus performs a check to make sure you don't have any issues. This is called the Preflight Verifier. (Also an icon, a pair of glasses left of the PDF icon.)

Whoops! We've got errors! In order to remove them, we need to find them!

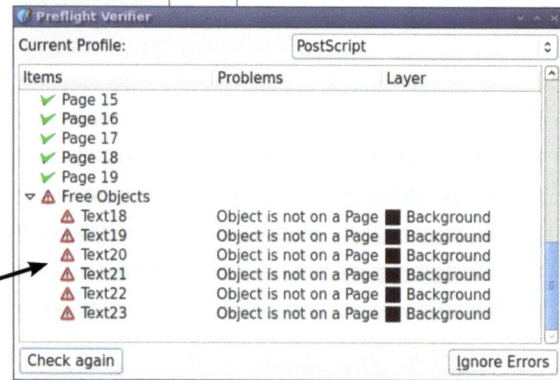

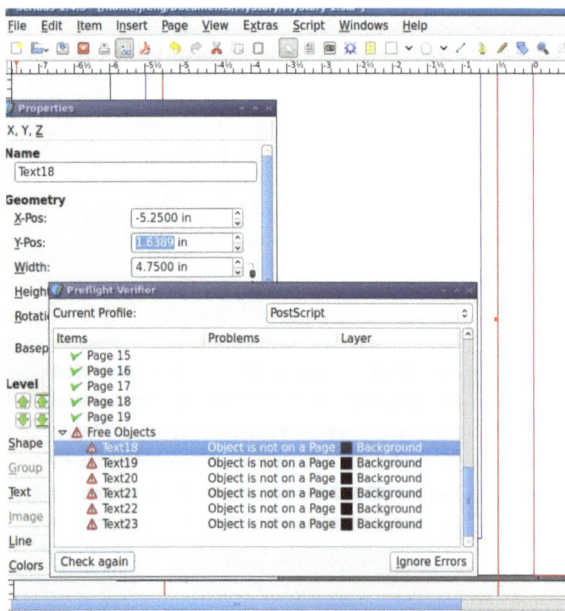

To find the problem and remove it, double-click the first item in the Preflight list. Make sure your Properties dialog is open (F2) and on X, Y, Z. Look for the name to match the problem object. In this case, it's Text18. Typically one Geometry setting will be wildly off. In this case, it was over 66! So we change it to 1 and it should show up, selected, somewhere on the screen. If not, page back and forward to find it. Then press Delete to remove it. Repeat for the remaining objects, then click *Check again* to recheck the document.

Once you have a clean list, like below, click *OK* to move on.

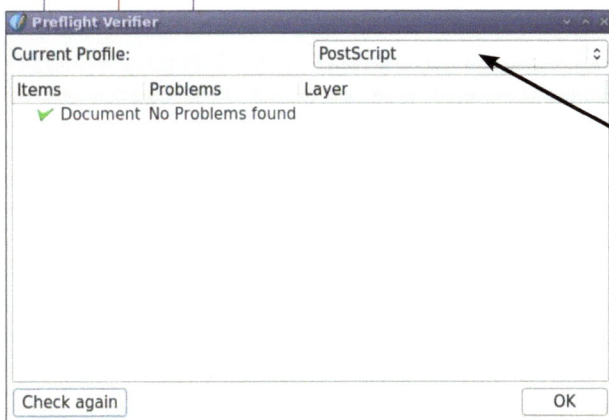

Notice the current profile on the Verifier defaults to Postscript. I haven't found that changing this gets different results. Now we can manage the PDF settings.

We'll check settings on 3 of the tabs and leave the others at the default.

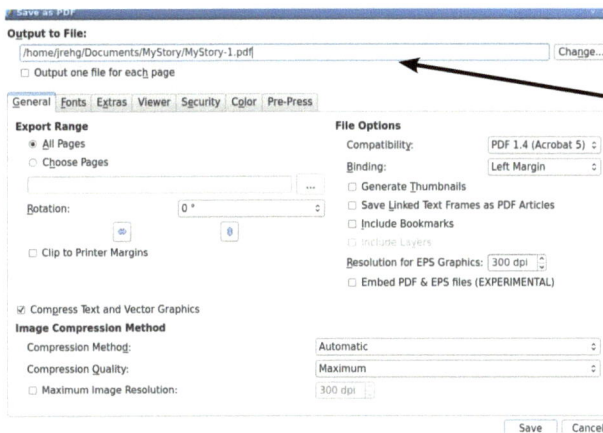

On the General tab, you can change your filename and directory if you don't like the default. Important here is Compatibility, under File Options, should be PDF 1.4.

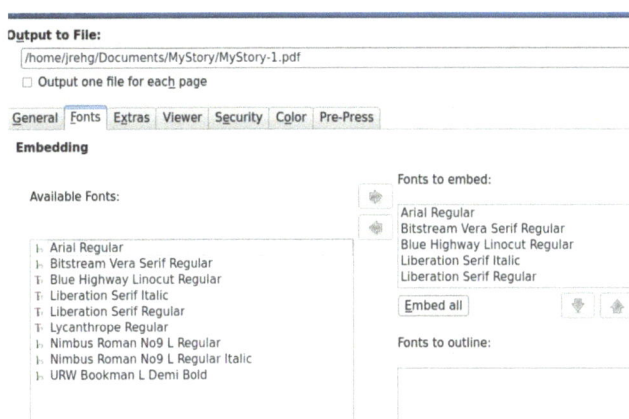

On the Fonts tab make sure to embed all your fonts. (Some will only outline.) Scribus handles most of this automatically.

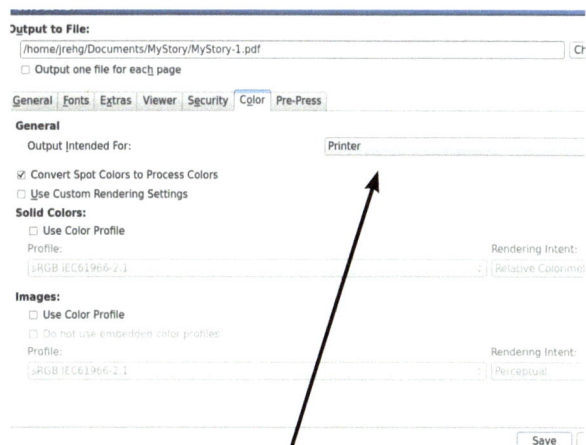

On the Color tab, set the Output Intended For to Printer, as this will be printed. Then click Save.

Recap

Fantastic! You've completed your interior file, created a pdf, and now only have to upload it to CreateSpace. Let's take a breath and review what you did.

- Styled your document in your word processor
- Set up styles and master pages in Scribus
- Imported your chapters and replaced the styles
- Set up your front pages
- Exported to PDF
- And most of all - completed your story!

Take another breath. You've done a great job! Way to go!

The Fine Print

This is a great moment. You've got a completed interior file for your print book. In an appendix, I'll cover converting your primary word processor file into an ebook in more detail, but you have another option there as well.

CreateSpace will convert your print book for you, for a price, into an ebook. It's that simple. You have a choice on some of these steps as to whether you will take the lowest cost option or the lowest effort one.

It's up to you. But if you made it this far, realize you've done the hardest part, and everything else is just a matter of options and effort.

Step 7
Build Your Cover and Export to PDF

Now you're at a decision point. Do you tackle a graphics program to create your cover, hire a specialist, or use CreateSpace's free Cover Creator?

If all you need is a basic cover, some words, maybe a picture, and a simple background, then by all means, consider using the free Cover Creator. I tested it once and had a cover complete in 5 minutes. It was that easy. You have a choice of designs and fonts. And if you are using a CreateSpace ISBN, then this might make even more sense.

If you want the most professional-looking cover, consider hiring a graphic artist who specializes in book covers. If you find the right person, you'll have a quality cover similar to what you find in bookstores. (Remember them?) But it can cost you. So shop around and ask for referrals.

Or, consider building your own. You're not artistic, right? No clue how to design a cover? Well, a simple one, while more work than the Cover Creator, gives you more control and flexibility over the end product. And once you get familiar with the program, you'll find you can do so much more.

Here, we'll just touch on the basics. Ready? I assume you've already installed GIMP.

Take a deep breath, and let's get started!

The Fine Print

GIMP. (GNU Image Manipulation Program) Not for the faint-hearted. When I first looked at the program, I sat staring at the screen wondering what to do. I started hunting online for tutorials so I could understand how to use the interface.

That's right. Even though I had some artistic background (but nothing like a graphic artist), and a deep computer background, I was completely at a loss.

I'm here to walk you through it step by step, keystroke by keystroke. I won't sugar coat it, it's not an easy program to get used to. Others have told me, use this one or that one instead, but they all have similar interfaces. It's not the program, it's understanding how they work. (Even the commercial ones have steep learning curves.)

GIMP

When you first start GIMP, you're presented with this.

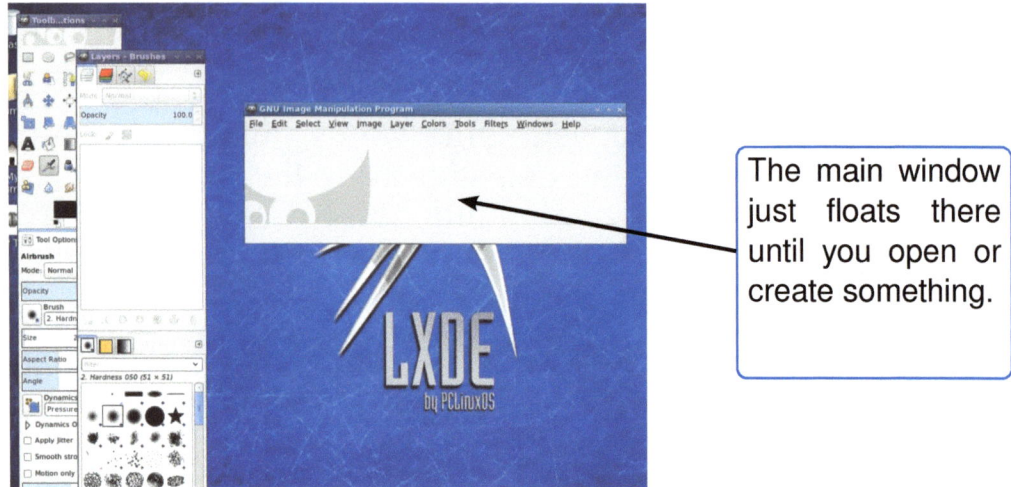

The main window just floats there until you open or create something.

What? Yeah, not a single screen interface, but a little horizontal one, with two floating palettes.

The key to understanding and using the program is to consider this: Everything is done in layers, as if you are putting transparent sheets of paper on top of each other. Once you understand that, you're halfway there.

Download the cover templates for your book size from CreateSpace.

The Fine Print

It took me hours of watching and stepping through tutorials, of starting over many times, before I finally got the hang of this program. I'll show you the things to watch out for (unless some bugs have been fixed), and how to navigate it to get the most out of it, on a basic level.

There are many fine tutorials and helpful websites, not least of which is the gimp.org forum. Without naming everyone, I'm grateful to them all.

We won't cover the fancier things - we'll basically do what Cover Creator does - but you'll gain the confidence to search out and learn new techniques once you've mastered the basics. (Or at least become familiar with them.) If you've gotten this far, and want complete control over your cover without paying a designer, then dig in!

CreateSpace Cover Template

This is your roadmap to building your cover. Select the size of your book (including page count, which you now have from Scribus), and unzip the file. It will contain 2 files, a pdf, and a png file (image). We'll use the image file.

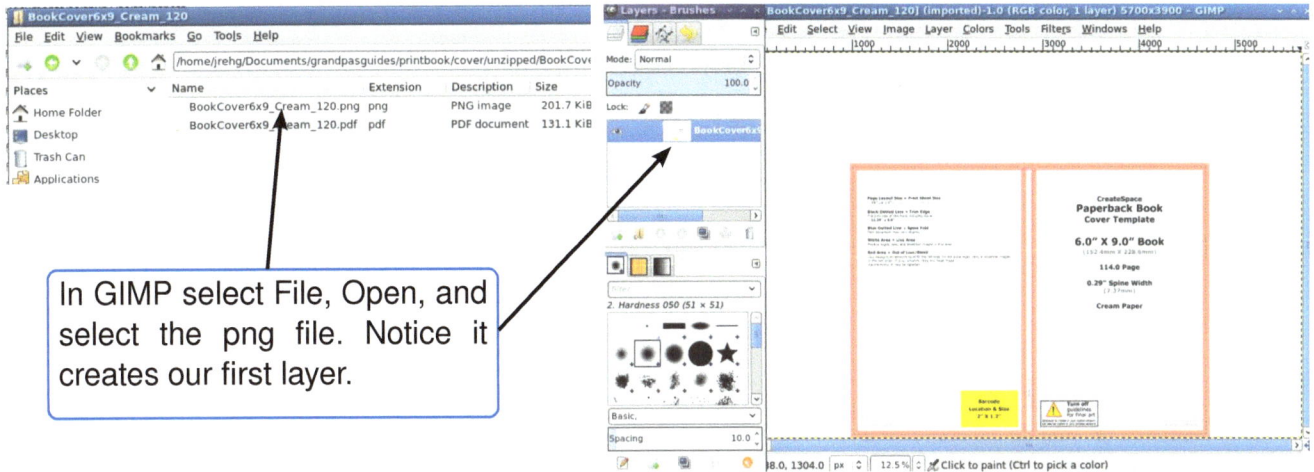

In GIMP select File, Open, and select the png file. Notice it creates our first layer.

Now we have the outline of our book cover. It includes the front, the back, and the spine. The width of the spine is dependent on how many pages you have. We're using one from Grandpa Tic's book, since the size is 6x9.

If you're planning an ebook, you'll get two for one, putting together the front first, saving it to another filename, and then completing the back for the print version. That way you have the same front cover for both editions.

The Fine Print

You might get confused with the layers approach, but stay with it and you'll gain an appreciation for it. It's really nice, because if you make a mistake on one layer, you just remove it and start that one over, without losing the rest of your work. For this reason, it's important to save different versions with each layer, so it's easy to backtrack if necessary.

When you get to the final product, you'll combine all the layers into one before exporting. Save that to a new filename so you'll still have a master with all the layers.

The good news is that you can design the front cover part one time and use it for both your print and ebook! (See? There is good news!)

Front Cover
Background Layer

Let's begin with the front cover, examining the template to see what it tells us. The outer colored boundary is the outer edge for our cover. CreateSpace (CS) will trim this to the dotted line in the middle of that boundary, so anything important should be in the inner white space.

First we'll create a solid color background to cover the front area. We'll add a new layer on top of this one, and size it just for the front. If you decide your entire cover will be this one color, then you'll want to size it over the entire template.

In fact, let's make this simple, with a solid background for the entire book. We'll crop out the back for the ebook. This way, we won't have to line up any color on the spine.

Select *Layer, New Layer* from the menu.

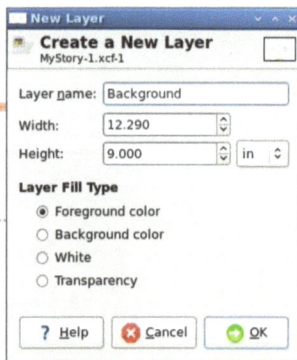

The Create a New Layer Dialog

We use the dimensions shown on the template, name our layer, and choose the foreground color.

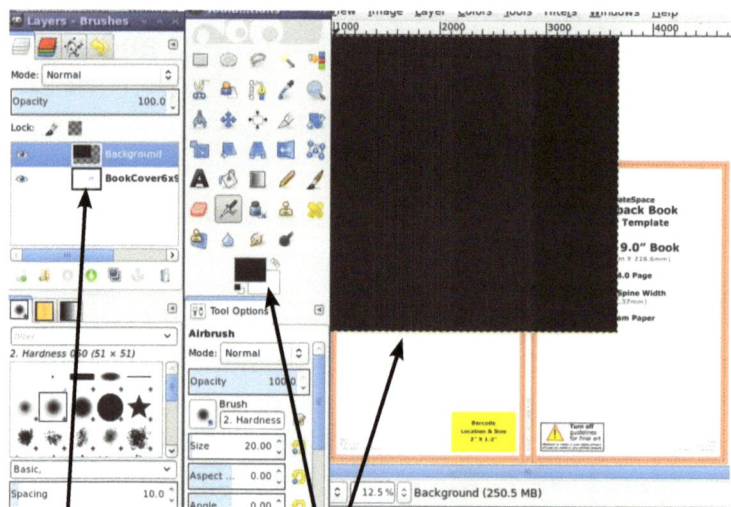

Notice the layer is positioned at the top left. We choose the foreground color from the palette.
Now the layers dialog shows 2 layers.

Drag the layer over to cover your template. Click on the Move icon (1) and select *Move the active layer* (2) at the bottom of the Toolbox palette.

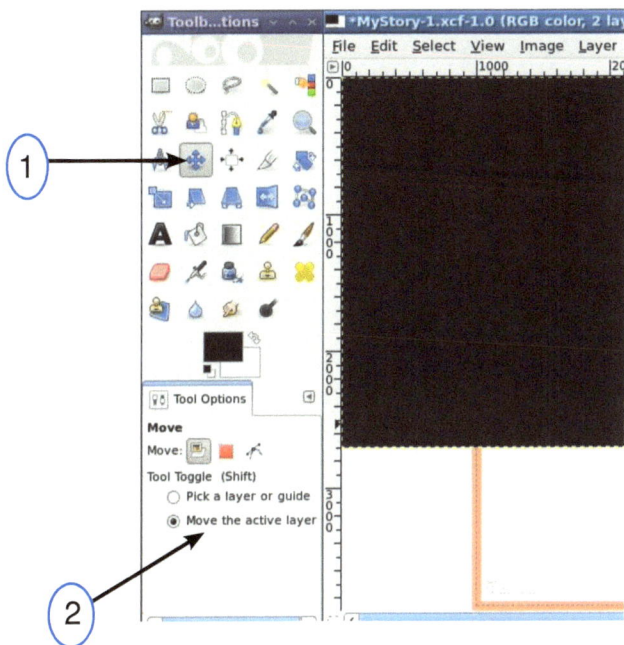

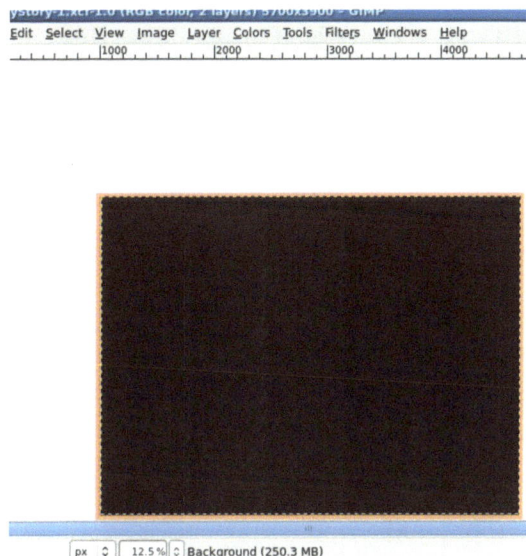

Click and drag the layer to the desired location.

Notice your layer doesn't quite cover the template. Now scale the layer to completely cover the colored edge of the template. Click on the scale icon (3), or select *Layer, Scale Layer.* (Shift+T) Move your mouse into one of the centered boxes that overlap a side, and click and drag the edge out to cover the template. You'll know you can drag when you see the mouse cursor change to an arrow pointing away from the center of the layer. When you complete your adjustments, click *Scale*.

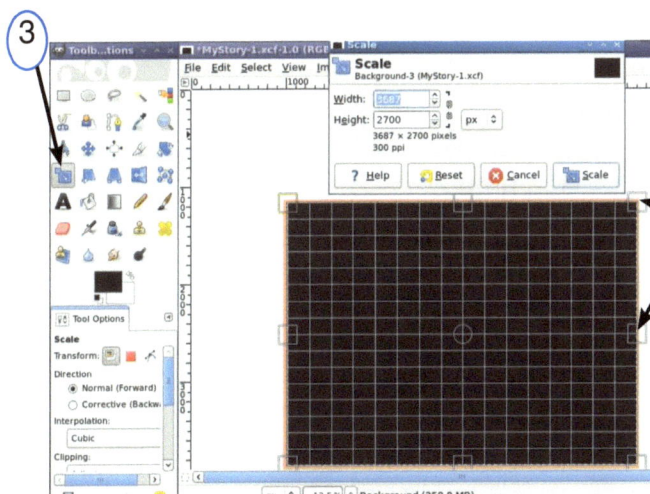

Drag from one of these handles to adjust a side, or two sides from a corner.

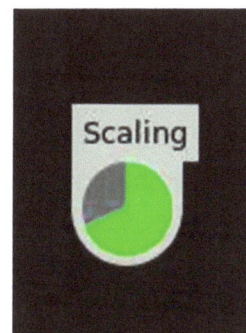

Preparing to Scale a Layer

The layer takes time to scale

Now you've got your layer set, but you can't see the template anymore to line up your other parts to the puzzle. No problem. You can make a layer invisible. Click the eye (4) to the far left of the layer name in the Layer dialog. Presto! The layer disappears. Press that area again, (revealing the eye) and it comes back. You can also zoom in and out quickly with the zoom at the bottom of the window. (What's usually called the status bar.)

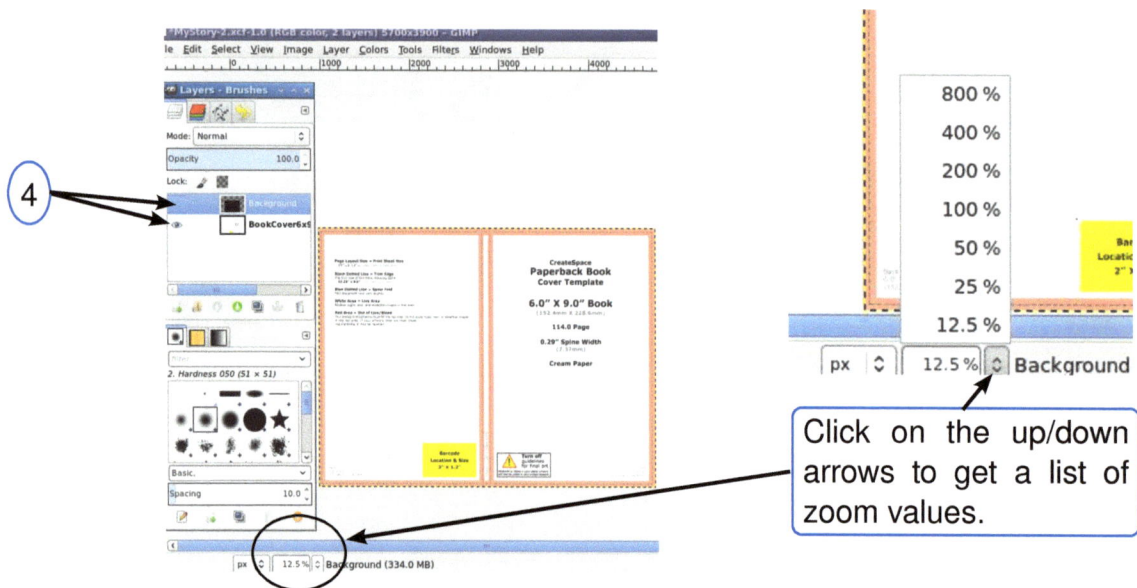

Click on the up/down arrows to get a list of zoom values.

Congratulations! Your first layer is in place.

The Fine Print

Was that so difficult? It was? Don't worry. With practice it gets easier.

The minimum number of layers for a cover is 6 (5 for thin books):
• Background color
• Front title
• Author name
• Spine title and author (if it's wide enough - CreateSpace will tell you)
• Back cover text (if just one block of text)
• ISBN/price barcode

Why? Each text block is its own layer. You can easily reach 10 layers if you add pictures on front and back, and multiple text blocks.

Front Cover
Picture Layer

Now let's add a picture on our front cover. You can get really fancy with this, but it takes following detailed tutorials that aren't included in this book. Here, we'll just add a picture to our front cover, without modifying it in any way. Before we do this, though, we'll want to make sure the picture is in high enough resolution for print, 300 dpi. (dpi = dots per inch, 300 is the minimum for print)

We'll open the picture file in GIMP separate from our cover file. The select *Image, Scale Image*, and note the resolution. Ours is too low, so we'll type in 300 in the X resolution field, press tab (which updates Y). Then change pixels to inches and press the Width up arrow twice. This creates a larger image which, when we compress it on our cover will increase the resolution above 300, keeping us safe. If you don't increase the size and then decide to increase it where you're using it, the resolution will drop below 300, making the image fuzzy in print.

Click *Scale* to scale the image.

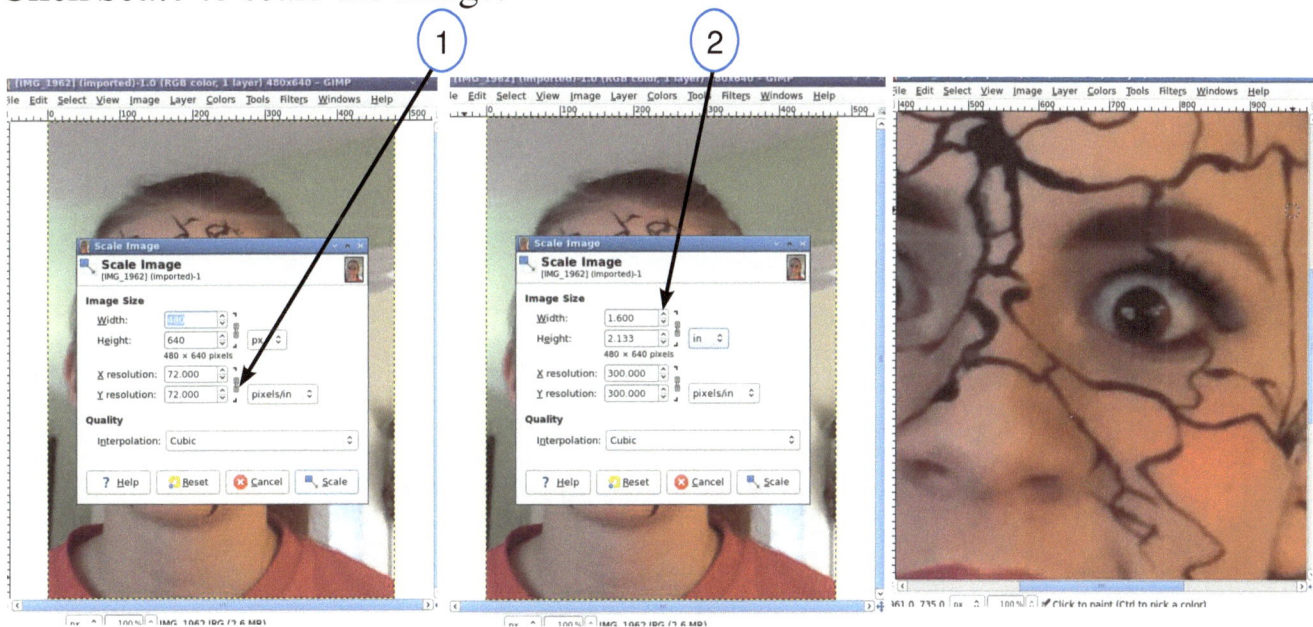

| Before adjustment - 72 dpi is too low for print | Change resolution to 300 | After scaling |

If after you type in 300 in the X resolution and press tab the Y resolution does not change, then your measurements aren't linked. Click on the chain links (1) to close them up. This will then link Width to Height so when you click the up arrow (2) both dimensions will increase proportionally. Note that we changed from px to in (inches) to better understand the size.

Now we'll save the image with a new name, indicating that this one is at our 300 dpi setting. You can scale higher, but for print it's not necessary. If we save in GIMP, it will give us a GIMP filename extension, which is unreadable by anything else. We want to save it as a picture, and we'll choose jpeg for our file format. So we're not really saving it, we're exporting it. Select *File, Export As*. (figure 1) Then type in the filename you want and click *Export*. The Export dialog pops up. (figure 2) I always push it to 100% (it defaults to 90), and if you want, under Advanced Options there's a subsampling quality that you can change to the highest. If you want the program to remember these, click *Save Defaults* after you've made your changes. Click *Export* to finish.

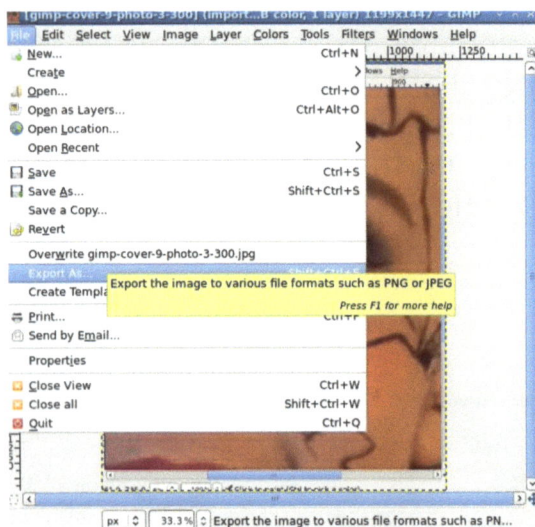

figure 1: Export As

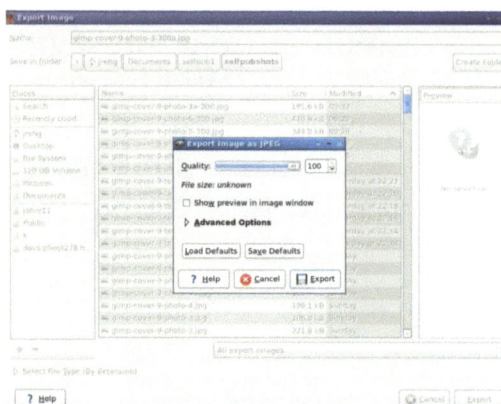

figure 2: Export dialog

The Fine Print

CreateSpace prints color at 300 dpi. You can save your cover higher than that, as long as it falls under the maximum size allowed.

One problem with what we just did, upscaling an image, is that it won't look as good as if the picture was taken at a higher resolution in the first place. If you notice any fuzziness in our images for this book, they were taken at 72 dpi as screenshots, then upscaled. If you think they are sharp enough, then that's great. You'll feel comfortable with upscaling a photo if need be.

When I upscale an image I export it and add -300 to the name so I know its resolution. Then I close the program and discard the changes, because I want to keep my original file in its original resolution.

Now we'll open the picture as a layer in our cover file. Select *File, Open as Layers*, and select your image file. This way, it opens in your cover rather than as a separate file. Then you need to place the image where you want it. Select the Move tool, and that you are moving the active layer. With the black background, it will be difficult to line up our picture where we want it, so we'll first make that layer invisible.

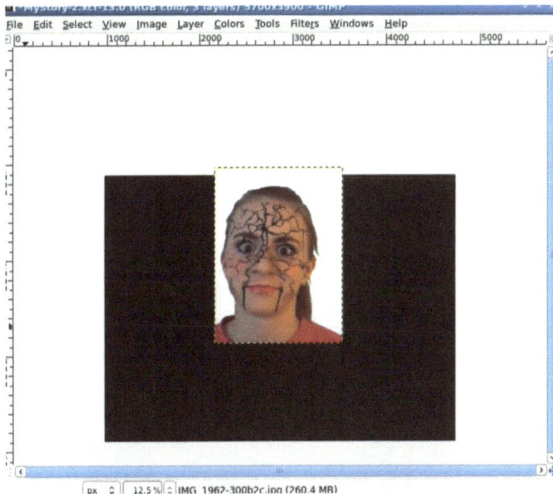

Open as Layers places the picture on our screen, but not where we want it.

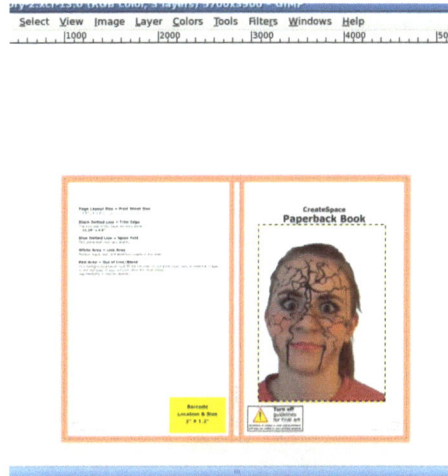

After turning off our background layer we are able to position the picture where desired.

Now let's add some text layers!

The Fine Print

If you choose a picture you can use 'as-is', then this is simple. If not, then it becomes much harder. Unless you're willing to spend hours on it, my recommendation is to let a professional do it, or find a different picture.

For our next set of images, I cropped the picture to show the person, then added more background to give it a texture. (I did this because I wasn't 100% successful in getting the picture cropped the way I wanted to - but in the end I liked the result.)

If you keep it simple, you can do it. Easily!

Front Cover
Title (Text) Layer

Each text block you create is a different layer. This is helpful in that you only have one font/color/size selection per layer. We'll create layers for the title, subtitle, and author name. That's 3 separate layers.

Select the Text tool (the big A on the palette, or *Tools, Text* from the menu, or press T on the keyboard). (below left) Then click and drag a rectangle to put your text in. (below right)

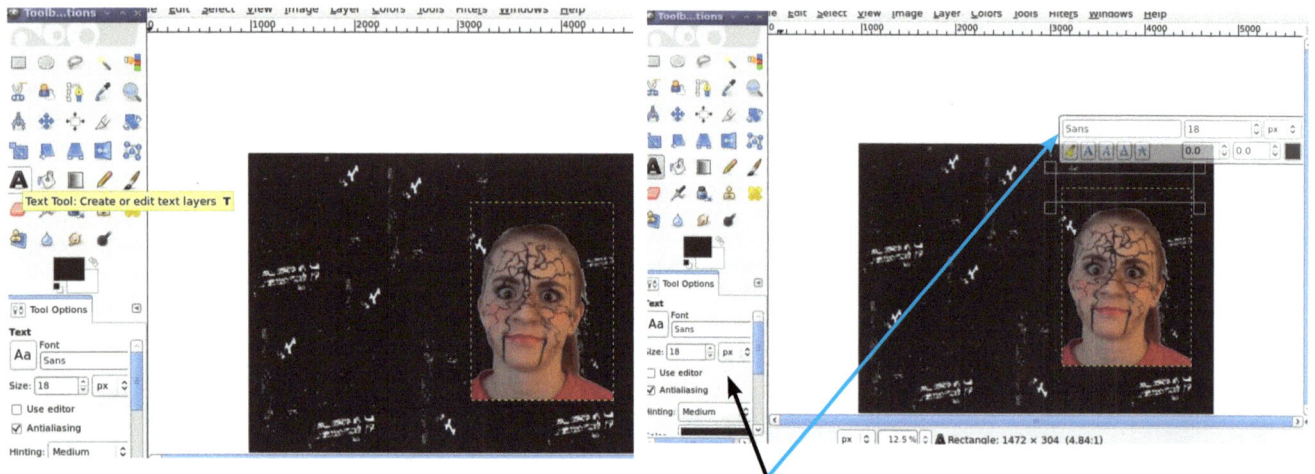

Which to use? The toolbox palette or the font palette that hovers over your image? I find the toolbox gives me greater control. Play with both to see how they behave differently. With the font palette, you have to select the text to make changes.

The Fine Print

The Text tool is one of the more frustrating tools to use, because of a bug. Sometimes selecting a different font suddenly closes the entire program. Because of this, I always save as often as possible when I'm creating text layers so I don't lose what I've done.

One way to avoid or minimize the occurrence of this behavior, is to select the font this way:

On the toolbox palette, highlight the font (default Sans) and begin typing the font you want. When you get the list where you can see the one you want, you can stop typing and select it with the mouse.

For the title I set my size to 150 first before I type anything. This gives me a good starting point, and after entering my text I'll adjust it to fit the cover. I highlight the font name and type in the one I want. Once you see it in the list you can stop typing and select it with the mouse. If you use the arrow keys, you may find the program closing on you.

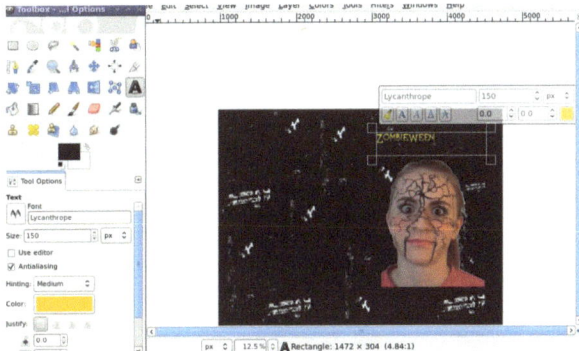

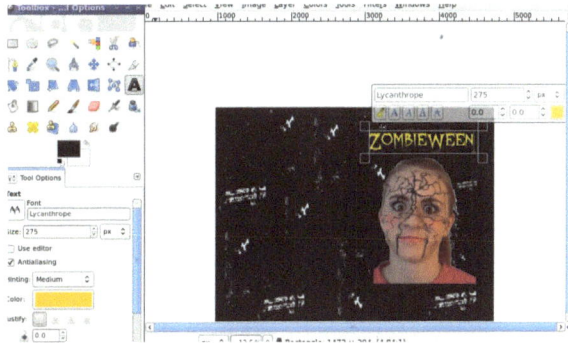

Notice 150 is too small. (above left) Using the Toolbox to increase the size means you don't have to select the text. If you use the Font palette, select the text first. I bump it up to 275. (above right) You may also have to resize the box, which you can do by placing your mouse on an edge until you get the arrow with the line, then clicking and dragging it to your desired dimensions.

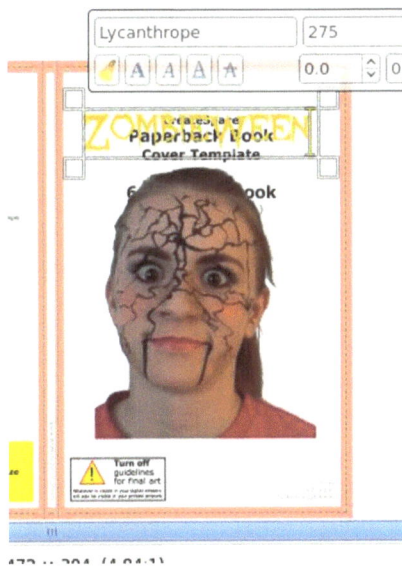

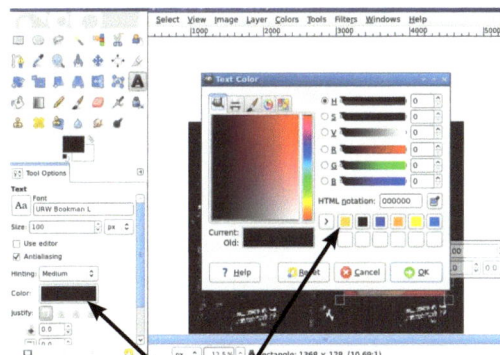

Hide the background layers to verify the alignment against the template.

To change colors, click on the color on the Toolbox and a Color palette will pop up, allowing you to set the color you want to use. If you want it to match a color you've already used, you can select from the row of blocks of previous colors.

You're almost done! Repeat the text layer steps, adding a layer for your subtitle (if you have one), and your author name. Save the file. Then save it again, for your ebook. Now we'll work with the ebook front cover.

Flatten the image into one layer. I do this by merging the layers down. Select the top layer. Then right-click and select *Merge down*. Continue doing this until you have one layer left.

Layers to compress. Notice the 1 layer in the bottom image.

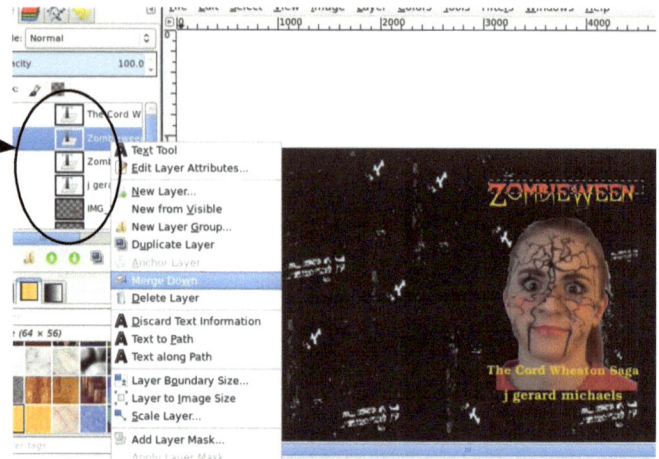

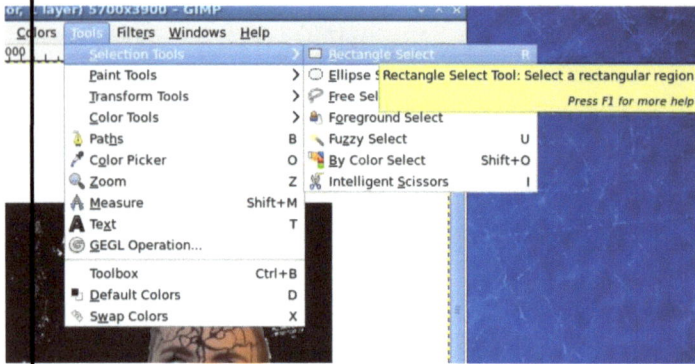

Then choose the Rectangle Selection tool (*Tools, Selection, Rectangle Select* or the rectangle on the Toolbox palette, or the letter R). Then click and drag to select the front part of your cover only (or close to it - you can always crop more later).

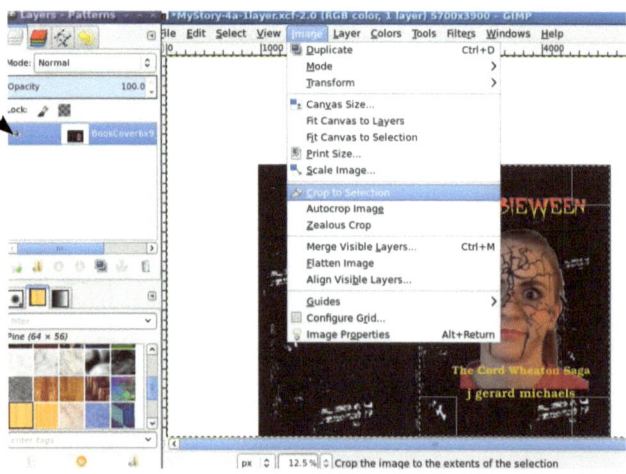

Now we'll choose *Image, Crop to Selection* from the menu. That will cut out everything else but what's inside our rectangle. We don't have to scale the image because it's already at 300 dpi, which is more than needed for the ebook (since it's on screen, it's resolution can be less, as low as 72 dpi).

When you're ready, you'll want to crop this cover to the dimensions preferred by Kindle, which are 1563 px wide by 2500 high.

Your ebook cover is complete. Now go back to your print cover file, and add your back cover text, spine text, and barcode (if you have your own ISBN). If CreateSpace is supplying your ISBN, leave that corner empty (of text).

To rotate your spine text, select the layer, then select the rotate tool (or Shift-R, or *Tools, Transform Tools, Rotate* from the menu). Then click on the text. Now enter -90 to set the text vertically.

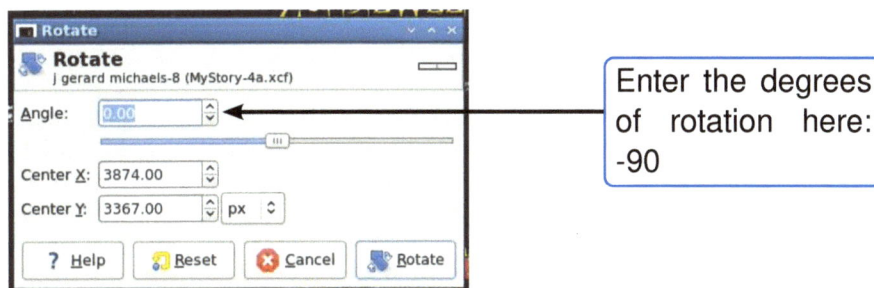

You can download software to create your barcode or use a service online that's free. There are several out there, try them and pick the one you like best. You'll do the same thing with your ISBN file as you did with your front cover picture, open as a layer, size and position it over the ISBN block on the back cover portion of the template.

The Fine Print

Congratulations! You've completed your covers for both print and ebook. You've completed your interior for print and if you followed the fine print after step 1, you've got an html file to upload as your ebook. You can upload your files for your print book.

Now you can create your upload files for the covers. They will be exported to different formats. For CreateSpace (print), export as PDF. For Kindle (ebook), export as jpeg. The jpg format we've already covered, so we'll look at what pops up when you export as pdf.

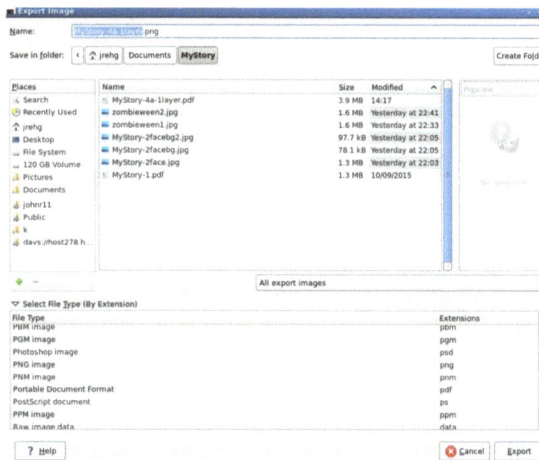

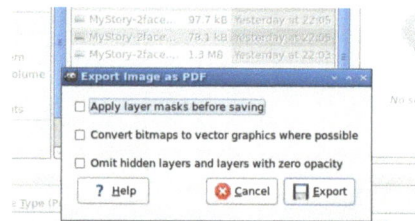

The PDF dialog - you can leave these unchecked.

Modify your filename, if desired. Then click *Select File Type (By Extension)* and scroll down to Portable Document Format (pdf) and click it. Then click Export.

The Fine Print

Take a deep breath and pat yourself on the back. You've done it!

Follow the directions on CreateSpace (print) and Kindle Direct Publishing (ebook) to upload your files.

For Kindle, you can preview your book online and if you need to make any corrections just modify your file and re-upload it. For CreateSpace, you can preview it online as well, but it's always good to order a proof first, and verify that everything lines up as you expect. If you need to make any changes, you can re-upload the file(s) and order another proof, or if it's minor, proof it online.

Bonus: Working with Images

With fiction, pictures or images are limited or non-existent. But if you have a memoir, especially one designed for the family, pictures are of paramount importance. We haven't really covered putting pictures in your book beyond a cursory statement. This bonus section remedies that, giving you the basics for inserting pictures, mostly in the white space at the end of a chapter, or on their own separate page(s). (Like an insert in the middle of the book.)

We covered upping the resolution on an image back in the front cover section of this book. Make sure your pictures or images are all at least 300 dpi (dots per inch) in resolution. If not, you can use GIMP or any photo program to increase it (though it won't look quite as good as if it had been taken originally at a higher resolution, in most cases it will work fine).

We'll insert pictures on a blank page. Go to a blank page and press the letter i. As you move your mouse over the page you'll see it's ready for you to click and drag an image frame on the page. (You can resize it later.)

Create your image frame. (below left) Then right click on the image frame and select *Get Image*. (below right) Or with the frame selected press *Ctrl-i*.

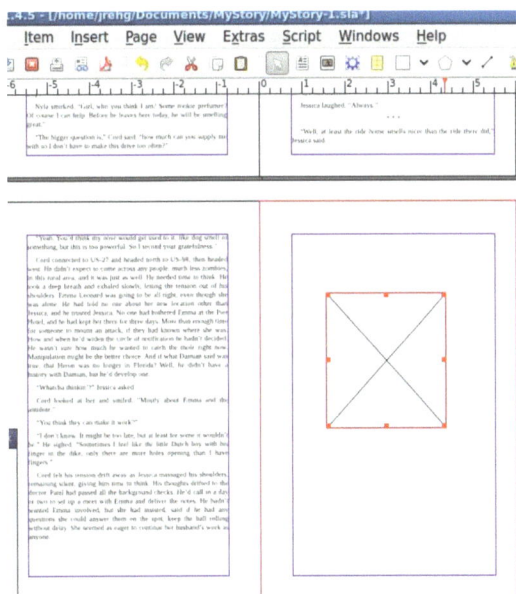

Image frame on a blank page

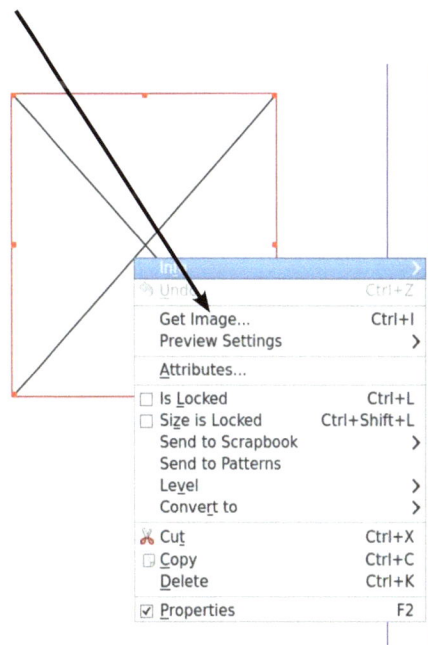

The Open Dialog box lets us select which image we want to put on the page. If you can see a preview of it, as we can here, it makes it easier to select the one you want (if you have a folder full of them, for instance). Click on the file you want so it's highlighted (below left), then click *OK* to put the image in the frame. (below right).

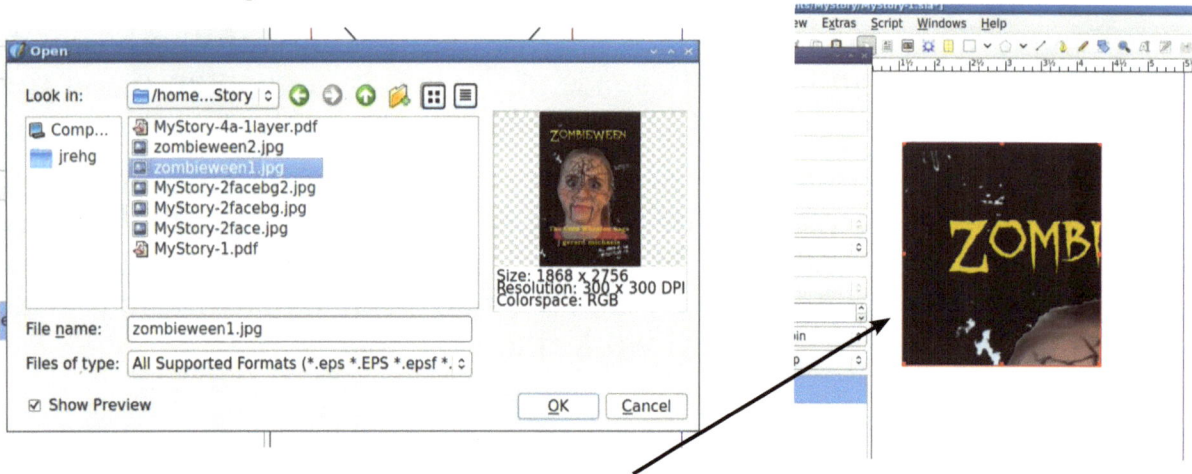

Notice we can't see much of the picture. We'll take 2 steps to get it situated, and from there we can move and resize it easily.

Right click on the image and from the dialog box that opens, first select *Adjust Image to Frame*. Then right click again and select *Adjust Frame to Image*.

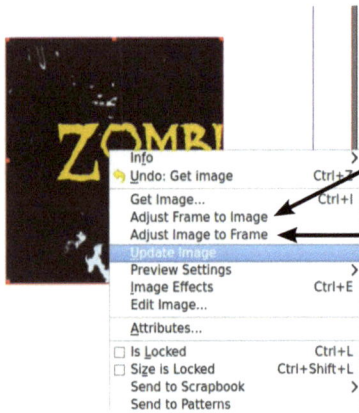

Step 1: click *Adjust Image to Frame*, then
Step 2: click *Adjust Frame to Image*

What does this do? The first step compresses the picture size. The second step sets the frame properly for later resizing.

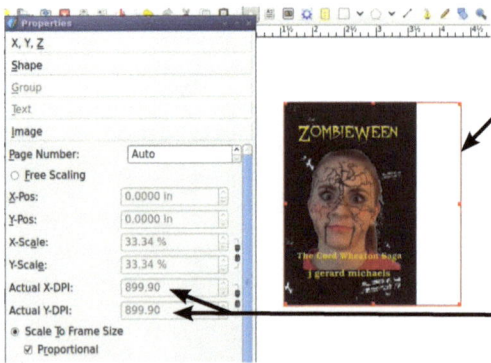

After step 1, the frame will be larger than the picture. Step 2 removes the extra space.
Notice the DPI. If you scaled correctly, these numbers will be higher than 300.

Frame is now at edge of image

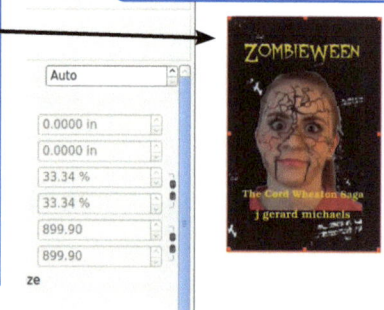

To change the size of an image, just grab one of the little red dots (left click and drag). If the frame size goes too big, repeat step 2 from the last page, re-adjusting the frame.

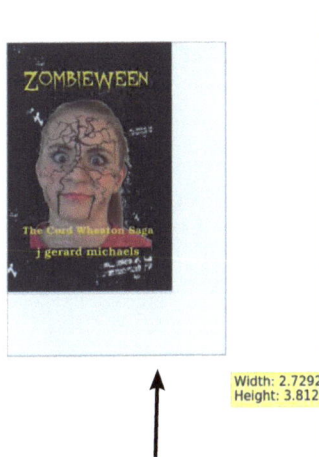

Width: 2.7292
Height: 3.812

Hold down left mouse button and drag the frame to your new size. Note the frame size is changing (though you can't see the mouse)

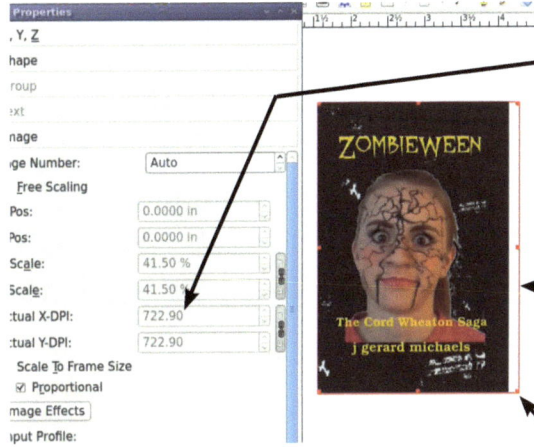

When you drag to a larger size, your resolution goes down. Make sure to keep it at 300 or higher.

DPI has dropped from 899 to 722. The image can be made much larger before it hits our 300 limit. We'll adjust the frame again once our size is set.

Use any of the 8 'handles' (little red squares) to size an image frame, just like with a text frame.

The Fine Print

Once you get the hang of it you'll be throwing in pictures quickly.
1. Insert an image frame (it can overlap a text frame, but let's keep it away from text)
2. Select your image (minimum 300 dpi resolution for print)
3. Adjust the image to the frame (this puts it at the size of the frame)
4. Adjust the frame to the image (removes white space around the image)
If you want to move the picture around, move your mouse inside the frame. When it changes into a hand, you can then left click and drag the picture around.

We'll cover one more basic feature, giving your pictures a little slant, a little personality!

Give your pictures a little personality by setting some of them at an angle. In the X, Y, Z section of the Properties, locate the Rotation and Basepoint items. The rotation sets how far you want to rotate your image, and the basepoint is what part of the image is held in place (a corner or the center). In the picture (below left) we have the top left corner held.

If we rotate 10 degrees (below right), the top left corner is still in the same position, and the image has come up on the right, as if the corner is pinned down and we're spinning the picture around the pin.

In the very bottom right, the degrees around a circle show how your picture will rotate. To move clockwise, go down from 360. Upside down is 180.

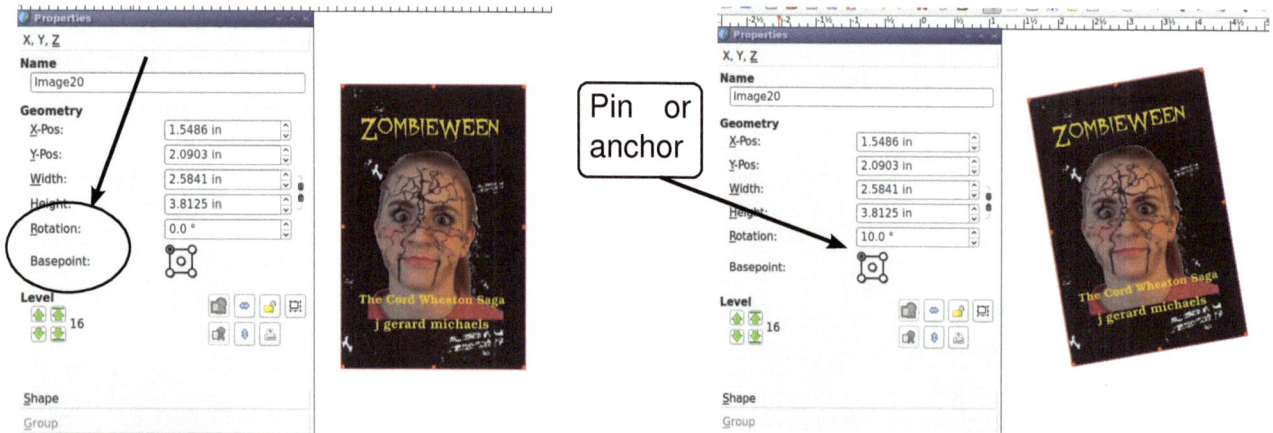

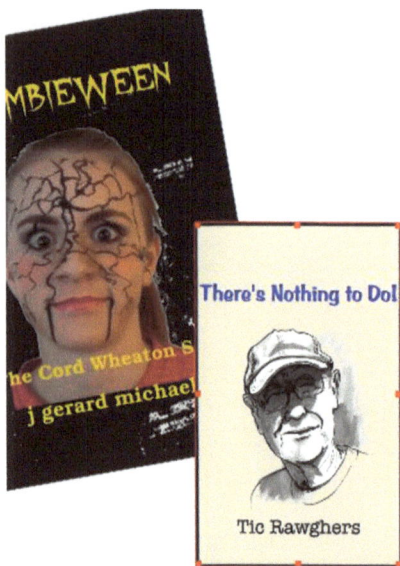

Put another picture on top

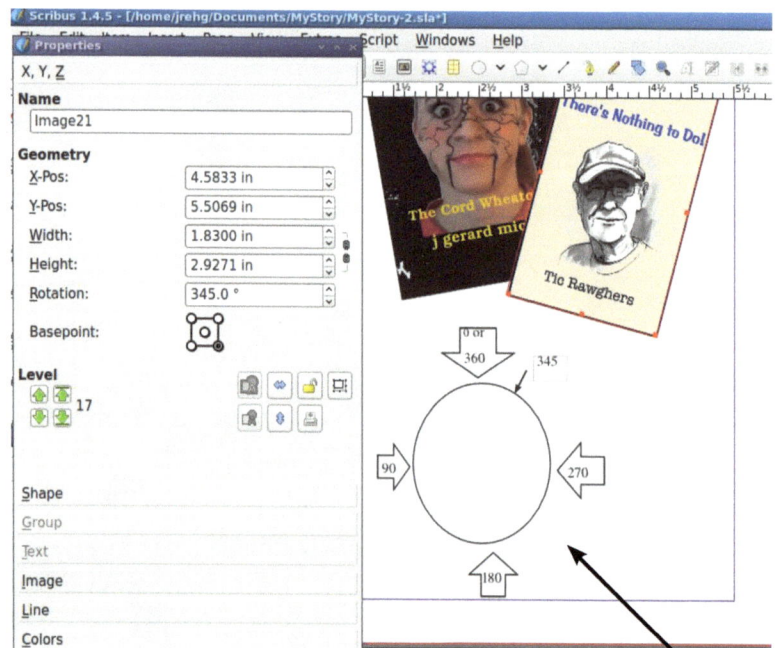

We anchor the 2nd picture on the bottom right, and rotate it 345 degrees! The circle with degree numbers shows how far it rotates for a given number. (There are 360 degrees in a circle.)

Self Publish for *FREE*

These are just the basics, which should be enough if you want to put pictures in the middle of your book, or at the end of a chapter. Places where they won't interfere with text.

I encourage you to play around with some of the other settings. You can do quite a bit (which we'll cover in a later book), and as long as you save your work before you change it, you can always get back to where you were.

Once again, here's how the rotation works: The picture spins counter-clockwise as the degrees of rotation increases. 90 degrees means you're laying the picture on its left side. 180 is turning it upside down, and 270 lays it on its right side. (270 is 90 degrees clockwise.)

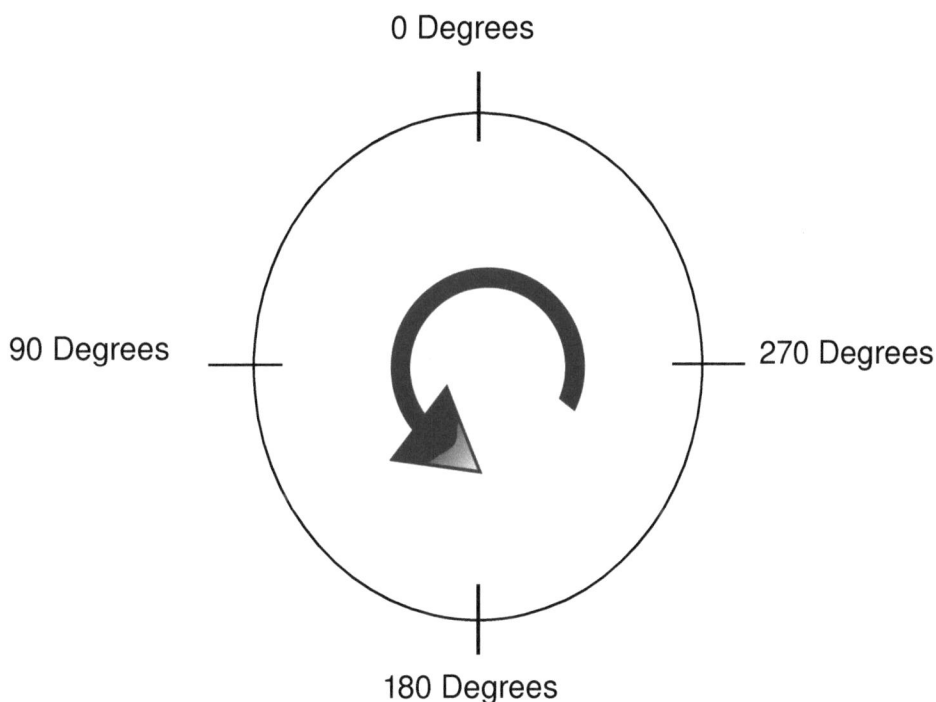

0 Degrees

90 Degrees

270 Degrees

180 Degrees

Acknowledgements

The following versions of software were used:

LibreOffice   Version: 5.0.1.2
Build ID: 81898c9f5c0d43f3473ba111d7b351050be20261
Locale: en-US (en_US.UTF-8)
The word processor program

Scribus   Version 1.4.5
26 January 2015
Build ID: C-C-T-F-C1.12.16
Using Ghostscript version 9.06
The layout program

GIMP   Version 2.8.14
The graphics program

Screenie   Version 1.0.4 written for PCLinuxOS-LXDE 2010
The screen capture program

PC Linux OS   LXDE 2015-1pclos2015
The operating system

The Fine Print

If you are using Windows or Mac systems, they come with their own screen capture programs built in, using specific key combinations. The three main programs are available on those platforms as well.

Fonts used in this book include Liberation and Nimbus, both open source and free.

We gratefully acknowledge the contributions of too many people to name. The open source community is a great place to learn how to use these programs, filled with many helpful people.